the
scrumptious
collection volume 1

Twenty delectable patterns for Fyberspates Scrumptious yarn
Garments and accessories to knit in luxurious silk and merino wool

Published by Fyberspates Ltd : 2011 : UK

the team

Publisher: Jeni Hewlett
Editor: Jen Arnall-Culliford
Art & Production Editor: Nic Blackmore
Photography: Amanda France
Pattern Designers: Jeni Hewlett
                                    Jen Arnall-Culliford
                                    Lily France
                                    Judy Furlong
                                    Elly Doyle
                                    Belinda Boaden
Models: Lily France
                                    Camilla Perkins

Technical Editing services: JenACKnitwear
Desktop Publishing services: Clear Impressions Ltd

First published in 2011 by Fyberspates Ltd
© Copyright Fyberspates Ltd 2011

Printed by Williams Press, Berkshire, UK

British Library Cataloguing in Publication Data:
a catalogue record for this book is available from
the British Library.
ISBN-978-0-9569008-0-7

Fyberspates Ltd
The Maintenance Room, The Nalder Estate, East
Challow, Near Wantage, Oxfordshire, OX12 9SY, UK

contents

 24

 26

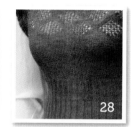 28

 31

scrumptious
lace

scrumptious
4ply/sport

 35

 36

 38

 40

 44

 45

 46

 49

scrumptious
dk/worsted

scrumptious
aran

 53

 54

 56

 57

 59

 60

 61

scrumptious
chunky

64

3

introduction

I'm very proud and happy that knitters far and wide find Scrumptious yarns a joy to knit with and to wear. Our delectable blend of silk and merino wool now comes in a full array of weights and a gorgeous selection of colours, and is available in shops all over the world. This collection of patterns is a natural progression for Fyberspates and the Scrumptious yarn range.

This book is something that was long overdue and which has been bubbling away in the back of my head for ages. So many people love Scrumptious and I'm very pleased that this collection of patterns will help you to transform those delicious squishy skeins of yarn into something fabulous and special.

Here at Fyberspates, we wanted to give you a collection of exceptional, fun and modern patterns, some of them perhaps even a little indulgent. It's been a great privilege to choose things that we *love* to go into this book, with nothing to hold us back. Our aim was to fill the book with ideas for everyone. Whether you want something quick, fun and instantly gratifying, or something complex and beautiful, it's all here, waiting for you to dive into the Scrumptious range and start knitting.

Bringing this book to life has been a joy from start to finish (hard work, yes, but joyous hard work). The thing that sets it apart from most is that it has been created by knitters. All the pattern designs, photography, technical editing, page design and layouts have been achieved with great love and attention to detail by knitters — even our beautiful models are knitters (admittedly, one slightly keener than the other!).

Every step of the process has involved passionate knitters — all of whom have knitted countless garments and accessories, from countless patterns and books, and all of whom understand the trials and tribulations that can be involved with following a knitting pattern.

Our hope is that the love with which the book was created will make each pattern a joy for you to knit.

Jeni

Jeni Hewlett
Fyberspates Ltd

www.fyberspates.co.uk

gallery

The Scrumptious Collection

Delicious original designs, for all skill levels

Each knitted in the divinely luxurious
blend of silk and finest merino wool
that is the Scrumptious yarn range

Burdrop
by Jeni Hewlett

shown in :
scrumptious lace
water

details :
page 24

A lighter-than-air laceweight cape. Each delicate layer ripples into the next for a vintage, feminine effect.

Hethe
by Judy Furlong

shown in :
scrumptious lace
rose pink

details :
page 31

A pretty, floaty, summer cardigan with an intricate lace and cable edging that glows in gorgeous pink.

Tirrold
by Jen Arnall-Culliford

shown in :
scrumptious lace
slate

details :
page 28

A versatile and smart fitted
top, ideal for work or
evening wear. Geometric lace
diamonds adorn the yoke.

Arncott
by Jen Arnall-Culliford

shown in :
scrumptious 4ply/sport
cherry

details :
page 36

A wonderful cabled hat, with clever crown decreases that create a gorgeous pattern reminiscent of a daisy.

Longcot
by Jeni Hewlett

shown in :
scrumptious aran
water

details :
page 57

A casual, comfortable jacket with a waterfall-front edge and textures to keep things interesting.

Filkins
by Jen Arnall-Culliford

shown in :
scrumptious aran
rose pink

details :
page 53

Quirky circles, knitted in three strips and joined together as you knit, to create an eye-catching wrap.

Murcott
by Jen Arnall-Culliford

shown in :
scrumptious dk/worsted
water

details :
page 49

Beautiful details, like the pleats at the front and centre back, punctuate this classic wrap-around cardigan.

Cogges
by Jeni Hewlett

shown in :
scrumptious chunky
magenta

details :
pages 59 and 60

*A chunky cabled hat and
armwarmers in vivid magenta
make a stylish statement
for chilly winter days.*

Sonning
by Jen Arnall-Culliford

shown in :
scrumptious lace
purple

details :
page 26

*This distinctive shawl is
perfect for those special
events where understated
elegance is essential.*

Wytham
by Jeni Hewlett

shown in :
scrumptious dk/worsted
teal

details :
page 46

*A versatile, flattering
cardigan that can be
dressed up or down
depending on the occasion.*

Uffington
by Jeni Hewlett

shown in :
scrumptious chunky
cherry

details :
page 61

*Chunky lace panels on
the front and back give
this lovely waistcoat real
character.*

Childry
by Elly Doyle

shown in :
scrumptious 4ply/sport
gold

details :
page 35

*A small shawl in the
Faroese tradition, with a
softly ruffled edge. Quick
and satisfying.*

Hendred
by Elly Doyle

shown in :
scrumptious dk/worsted
purple

details :
pages 44 and 45

*A flattering hat and fun
mittens will keep you
warm and toasty on brisk
autumn mornings.*

Stonor
by Belinda Boaden

shown in :
scrumptious 4ply/sport
teal

details :
page 40

The ideal cardigan for summer evenings. Lace and cables, shaped with a deep ribbed edge.

Chinnor
by Jen Arnall-Culliford

shown in :
scrumptious aran
moss and rose pink

details :
page 56

*Pretty stripes and a
simple pattern mean this
cowl stands out from
the crowd.*

Hinksey
by Lily France

shown in :
scrumptious aran
moss

details :
page 54

*Unusual cables give these
lovely mittens a stunning
sculpted look.*

Alvescot
by Jeni Hewlett

shown in :
scrumptious chunky
biscuit

details :
page 64

*Intricate lace decorates
this fitted, long-line
sweater with cables adding
an elegant, vintage touch.*

Challow
by Jeni Hewlett

shown in :
scrumptious 4ply/sport
midnight and water

details :
page 38

*Butterflies circle around
the yoke of this casual
sweater - just perfect for
leisurely weekends.*

the patterns

Burdrop

by Jeni Hewlett

A vintage-style cape of delicately layered ruffles.

Skills

Increasing, decreasing and knitting two sets of stitches together

Size

One size only
Width at top of first ruffle: approx 115cm (45½in)
Width at collar, gathered by ribbon: 24cm (9½in)
Length: approx 45cm (17½in)

Yarn

Fyberspates Scrumptious Lace (45% silk, 55% merino; 100g skeins)
Water (504) 2 x 100g skeins

Needles and accessories

1 set 2.75mm (UK12/US2) circular needles, 80-100cm long
1 set 3mm (UK11/US2-3) circular needles, 80-100cm long
A spare 2.75mm (UK12/US2) circular needle, 80-100cm long
Stitch markers (approx 13)
Ribbon, approx 1m

Tension

30 sts and 44 rows to 10cm over st st using 2.75mm needles – tension is not vital, as the cape simply drapes over the shoulders.

Abbreviations

Standard abbreviations appear on page 71.

Pattern notes

The cape is worked from the bottom up. Each ruffle is knitted separately and then joined to the cape by a row where stitches from the two pieces are knitted together. This is not a difficult pattern, it just involves a lot of knitting!

First ruffle

Using 3mm needles, loosely cast on 660 sts, placing markers after every 50 sts to help you to keep count.
Change to 2.75mm needles.
Starting with a knit row, work 28 rows in st st.
Next row (RS): K2tog across entire row. 330 sts.
Next row (WS): Purl.
Place sts on a spare circular needle.

Cape body

Using 3mm needles, loosely cast on 660 sts, placing markers every 50 sts to help you to keep count.
Change to 2.75mm needles.
Starting with a knit row, work 28 rows in st st.
Next row (RS): K2tog across entire row. 330 sts.
Next row (WS): Purl.
Work 28 more rows in st st.
Next row (RS joining row): Hold ruffle on spare needle, with RS facing, in front of needle with cape body sts and knit across row, knitting each stitch from the front needle together with a stitch from the rear needle. 330 sts.
Next row: Purl.
Work 26 more rows in st st.
Next row (dec): K4, *K2tog, K8; rep from * 31 more times, K2tog, K4. 297 sts.
Next row: Purl.
Place sts on spare circular needle and make second ruffle as follows.

Second and third ruffles

**Using 3mm needles, loosely cast on 594 sts, placing markers to help you to keep count as before.
Change to 2.75mm needles.
Starting with a knit row, work 28 rows in st st.
Next row (RS): K2tog across entire row. 297 sts.
Next row (WS): Purl.
Next row (RS joining row): Hold ruffle, with RS facing, in front of needle with cape body sts and knit across row, knitting each stitch from the front needle together with a stitch from the rear needle. 297 sts.
Next row: Purl.**
Work 28 more rows in st st.
Place sts on spare circular needle.

Add a third ruffle by working from ** to ** once more.
Work 26 more rows in st st.
Next row (dec): K4, *K2tog, K7; rep from * 31 more times, K2tog, K3. 264 sts.
Next row: Purl.
Place sts on a spare circular needle.

Fourth ruffle

Using 3mm needles, loosely cast on 528 sts, using markers to help you keep count again.
Change to 2.75mm needles and starting with a knit row, work 28 rows in st st.
Next row: K2tog across entire row. 264 sts.
Next row (WS): Purl.
Next row (RS joining row):
Hold fourth ruffle with RS facing in front of needle with cape body sts and knit across row, knitting each stitch on the front needle together with a stitch from the rear needle. 264 sts.
Next row: Purl.
Work 11 more rows in st st.
Next row (dec): K3, *K2tog, K6; rep from * 31 more times, K2tog, K3. 231 sts.
Work 11 more rows in st st.
Next row (dec): K3, *K2tog, K5; rep from * 31 more times, K2tog, K2. 198 sts.
Next row: Purl.
Place sts on a spare circular needle.

Fifth ruffle

Using 3mm needles loosely cast on 396 sts.

Change to 2.75mm needles and starting with a knit row, work 24 rows in st st.

Next row (dec): K2tog across row. 198 sts.

Next row: Purl.

Next row (RS joining row): Hold fifth ruffle with RS facing in front of needle with cape body sts and knit across row, knitting each stitch on the front needle together with a stitch from the rear needle. 198 sts.

Next row: Purl.

Next row (dec): K2, *K2tog, K4; rep from * 31 more times, K2tog, K2. 165 sts.

Work 3 rows in st st.

Next row (dec): K2, *K2tog, K3; rep from * 31 more times, K2tog, K1. 132 sts.

Next row: Purl.

Next row: KFB into every stitch. 264 sts.

Work 6 more rows in st st.

Change to 3mm needles and cast off all sts loosely.

Front edges

Using 2.75mm needles and with RS facing, starting at bottom edge of Right Front, pick up and knit 2 sts across every 3 rows, ending at final decrease row at neck. Approx 120 sts.

Next row (WS): PFB in every stitch. Approx 240 sts.

Work 6 more rows in st st.

Change to 3mm needles and cast off all sts loosely.

Using 2.75mm needles and with RS facing, starting at final decrease row of neck on Left Front, pick up and knit 2 sts across every 3 rows, ending at bottom edge. Approx 120 sts.

Complete Left Front edging as for Right Front edging.

Finishing

Block gently to measurements and weave in all ends. Pin ruffles out and spray them to minimise curling.

Sew ribbon to WS along final decrease row of neck, leaving two ends to use as ties. You can adjust the fit by changing how much you gather the neckline as you sew the ribbon to the knitted fabric. The sample has the ribbon sewn to give a collar width of 24cm.

Sonning

by Jen Arnall-Culliford

An elegant evening shawl with an intriguing shape.

Pattern notes
The two side triangles are knitted first – they are mirror images of each other. They are joined together with a delicate lace and twisted stitch panel – at the end of each row, one side triangle stitch is knitted together with a panel stitch. This joins the pieces together.

Right triangle
Cast on 2 sts.
Row 1 (RS): KFB twice. 4 sts.
Row 2 (WS): K4.
Row 3: K1, KFB twice, K1. 6 sts.
Row 4: K6.
Row 5: K3, yo, K3. 7 sts.
Row 6: K3, P1, K3.
Row 7: K3, yo, K1, yo, K3. 9 sts.
Row 8: K3, P3, K3.
Row 9: K3, yo, SSK, pm, K1, yo, pm, K3. 10 sts.
Row 10 (and all following WS rows): K3, slm, purl to marker, slm, P2, K3.
Row 11: K3, yo, SSK, slm, knit to marker, yo, slm, K3.
Rep last 2 rows until you have 124 sts between the markers.
You may find it helpful to place markers for every 10 sts increased in the central stocking stitch portion – this will save you from having to count the number of sts too often.
Work 1 more WS row and break yarn. Place these sts on a holder.

Left triangle
Cast on 2 sts.
Row 1 (RS): KFB twice. 4 sts.
Row 2 (WS): K4.
Row 3: K1, KFB twice, K1. 6 sts.
Row 4: K6.
Row 5: K3, yo, K3. 7 sts.
Row 6: K3, P1, K3.
Row 7: K3, yo, K1, yo, K3. 9 sts.
Row 8: K3, P3, K3.
Row 9: K3, pm, yo, K1, pm, K2tog, yo, K3. 10 sts.
Row 10 and all foll WS rows: K3, P2, slm, purl to marker, slm, K3.
Row 11: K3, slm, yo, knit to marker, slm, K2tog, yo, K3.
Rep last 2 rows until you have 124 sts

Skills
Lace with a knitted-on centre panel

Size
Wingspan approx 160cm (63in), relaxed after blocking
Nape of neck to bottom edge approx 62cm (24½in)

Yarn
Fyberspates Scrumptious Lace (45% silk, 55% merino; 100g skein)
Purple (505) 1 x 100g skein

Needles and accessories
1 pair 2.75mm (UK 12/US 2) knitting needles (you may need circular needles, due to the number of sts)
Stitch holder or waste yarn
Stitch markers

Tension
Gently blocked: approx 29 sts and 36 rows to 10cm over stocking stitch

Special abbreviations
Wrap With yarn in back, slip the number of sts stated to RH needle, take yarn to front, slip the sts back to LH needle, take yarn to back and slip the same number of sts to RH needle. These sts will now be wrapped with yarn – they aren't knitted on this row. Standard abbreviations appear on page 71.

between the markers.
You may find it helpful to place markers for every 10 sts increased in the central stocking stitch portion – this will save you from having to count the number of sts too often.
Work 1 more WS row and *do not* break yarn.

Central panel
With RS facing, and left triangle sts on LH needle, using the attached yarn, cast on 69 sts.
Next row (RS): K68, pm, K2tog, turn. Leave the remaining left triangle sts unworked.
Next row (WS): Sl 1, slm, K67, pm, Sl 1, with WS facing, place right triangle sts on RH needle, Sl first triangle stitch to LH needle, K2tog tbl, turn leaving remaining right triangle sts unworked.
Next row (RS): Sl 1, slm, K67, slm, K2tog, turn.
Next row (WS): Sl 1, slm, K67, slm, SSK, turn.
Work last 2 rows once more.
In the foll section the st patt between markers is also shown on the chart.
Row 1 (RS): Sl 1, slm, K1, *yo, [K1 tbl, P3] 5 times, K1 tbl, yo, K1; rep from * twice more, slm, K2tog, turn. 73 sts between markers.
Row 2 (WS): Sl 1, slm, P3, *[K3, P1] 4 times, K3, P5; rep from * once more, [K3, P1] 4 times, K3, P3, slm, P2tog tbl, turn.
Row 3: Sl 1, slm, K1, *yo, K1 tbl, yo, [K1 tbl, P3] 5 times, [K1 tbl, yo] twice, K1; rep from * twice more, slm, K2tog, turn. 85 sts between markers.
Row 4: Sl 1, slm, P5, *[K3, P1] 4 times, K3, P9; rep from * once more, [K3, P1] 4 times, K3, P5, slm, P2tog tbl, turn.
Row 5: Sl 1, slm, K1, *yo, K1 tbl, yo, SSK, yo [K1 tbl, P2tog, P1] 5 times, K1 tbl, yo, K2tog, yo, K1 tbl, yo, K1; rep from * twice more, slm, K2tog, turn. 82 sts between markers.
Row 6: Sl 1, slm, P7, *[K2, P1] 4 times, K2, P13; rep from * once more, [K2, P1] 4 times, K2, P7, slm, P2tog tbl, turn.
Row 7: Sl 1, slm, K1, *K1 tbl, [yo, SSK]

twice, yo, [K1 tbl, P2] 5 times, K1 tbl, yo, [K2tog, yo] twice, K1 tbl, K1; rep from * twice more, slm, K2tog, turn. 88 sts between markers.

Row 8: Sl 1, slm, P8, *[K2, P1] 4 times, K2, P15; rep from * once more, [K2, P1] 4 times, K2, P8, slm, P2tog tbl, turn.

Row 9: Sl 1, slm, K2, *[yo, K2tog] twice, yo, K1 tbl, yo, [K1 tbl, P2tog] 5 times, [K1 tbl, yo] twice, [SSK, yo] twice, K3; rep from * once more, [yo, K2tog] twice, yo, K1 tbl, yo, [K1 tbl, P2tog] 5 times, [K1 tbl, yo] twice, [SSK, yo] twice, K2, slm, K2tog, turn. 85 sts between markers.

Rows 10 & 12: Sl 1, slm, P10, *[K1, P1] 4 times, K1, P19; rep from * once more, [K1, P1] 4 times, K1, P10, slm, P2tog tbl, turn.

Row 11: Sl 1, slm, SSK, *[yo, K2tog] 3 times, K1 tbl, yo, [K1 tbl, P1] 5 times, K1 tbl, yo, K1 tbl, [SSK, yo] 3 times, Sl 2 as if to knit 2 together, K1, p2sso; rep from * once more, [yo, K2tog] 3 times, K1 tbl, yo, [K1 tbl, P1] 5 times, K1 tbl, yo, K1 tbl, [SSK, yo] 3 times, K2tog, slm, K2tog, turn.

Row 13: Sl 1, slm, K1, *[K2tog, yo] twice, K2tog, K1, K1 tbl, yo, [SSK] twice, Sl 1, K2tog, psso, [K2tog] twice, yo, K1 tbl, K1, SSK, [yo, SSK] twice, K1; rep from * twice more, slm, K2tog, turn. 67 sts between markers.

Row 14: Sl 1, slm, wrap 2, *P7, wrap 5, P7, wrap 3; rep from * once more, P7, wrap 5, P7, wrap 2, slm, P2tog tbl, turn.
Rows 1 to 14 set the central panel pattern repeat. With each repeat you will use up 7 of the triangle sts on each side. Continue to work in pattern for a further 238 rows (18 repeats in total).

Next row (RS): Sl 1, slm, K67, slm, K2tog, turn.

Next row (WS): Sl 1, slm, K67, slm, SSK, turn.
Work these two rows twice more.
Cast off 69 sts very loosely.

Finishing

Weave in all ends but do not trim. Soak shawl in tepid water for 20 minutes. Squeeze gently and place between towels. Press to remove excess water. Lay a large towel on a flat surface, into which you can pin (carpet or foam tiles work well). Spread out the shawl to measurements and using pins, or pins and wires, pin out the shawl and leave to dry thoroughly. When completely dry, unpin and trim ends.

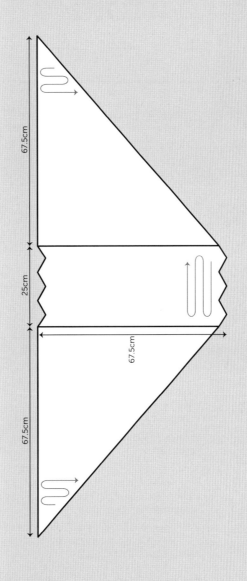

Key

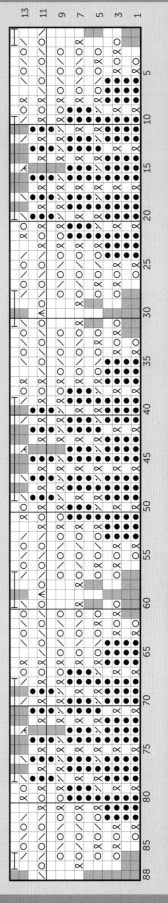

● Purl on RS, Knit on WS

ᚱ K1 tbl on RS

╲ SSK on RS

╱ K2tog on RS

⟋ P2tog on RS

⅄ Sl 1, K2tog, psso

Ⱄ Sl 2 as if to K2tog, K1, p2sso

O Yarnover

▨ No stitch, ignore these squares and move straight to next knitting instruction

⊢ Wrap the number of stitches covered by the symbol (don't count no stitch squares)

Tirrold

by Jen Arnall-Culliford

A smart sleeveless lace top — perfect for summer.

Skills

Lace and working in the round

Size

To fit bust

8	10	12	14	16	18	20	22	
81	**86**	**91**	**97**	**102**	**107**	**112**	**117**	cm
32	34	36	38	40	42	44	46	in

Actual bust

77	82	87	93	98	103	108	113	cm
30½	32	34	36½	38½	40½	42½	44½	in

Actual length – short version (shown)

45	45	47	47	49	49	51	51	cm
17½	17½	18½	18½	19½	19½	20	20	in

Actual length – long version

50	50	52	52	54	54	56	56	cm
19½	19½	20½	20½	21¼	21¼	22	22	in

Yarn

Fyberspates Scrumptious Lace (45% silk, 55% merino; 100g skeins) Slate (506)

Short version, all sizes
1 x 100g skein

Long version
1 (1, 1, 1, 1, 1, 2, 2) x 100g skeins

Needles and accessories

1 set each of 2.5mm (UK 12-13/US 1-2), 2.75mm (UK 12/US 2), 3mm (UK 11/US 2-3) circular needles, 60-80cm
1 pair 2.75mm (UK 12/US 2) knitting needles
Stitch markers

Tension

Relaxed, after firm blocking: 29 sts and 46 rounds to 10cm over st st using 2.75mm needles
30 sts and 56 rounds to 10cm over fully stretched rib using 2.5mm needles
1 repeat of lace pattern measures 7.5cm wide after blocking

Body

Using 3mm circular needles and the long-tail method, loosely cast on 192 (208, 224, 236, 252, 268, 284, 296) sts, and join to work in the round taking care not to twist the sts. Place marker for start of round.
Change to 2.5mm needles.
Round 1: *K2, P2; rep from * to end of round.
Last round sets rib patt.

SHORT VERSION ONLY

Repeat last round 83 (83, 89, 89, 89, 89, 89, 89) more times.
When firmly stretched out, rib should measure 15 (15, 16, 16, 16, 16, 16, 16) cm.

LONG VERSION ONLY

Repeat last round 111 (111, 117, 117, 117, 117, 117, 117) more times.
When firmly stretched out, rib should measure 20 (20, 21, 21, 21, 21, 21) cm.

ALL SIZES

Change to 2.75mm needles.
Next round: Knit.
Last round sets st st in the round.
Repeat last round 11 more times.
Next round (inc): *K1, M1, K94 (102, 110, 116, 124, 132, 140, 146), M1, K1, pm; rep from * once more. 196 (212, 228, 240, 256, 272, 288, 300) sts.
Knit 2 rounds, slipping markers as you reach them.
Next round (inc): *K1, M1, knit to 1 st before next marker, M1, K1, slm; rep from * once more. 200 (216, 232, 244, 260, 276, 292, 304) sts.
Knit 2 rounds, slipping markers as you reach them.
Repeat last 3 rounds 6 more times. 224 (240, 256, 268, 284, 300, 316, 328) sts.
Knit 10 (10, 10, 10, 16, 16, 20, 20) more rounds without further shaping.
Repeat inc round only 8 more times. 256 (272, 288, 300, 316, 332, 348, 360) sts.
Place markers to show start of armhole.

Back

Next row (RS): K3 (7, 0, 3, 7, 1, 5, 8) work Chart Row 1, repeating marked section 5 (5, 6, 6, 6, 7, 7, 7) times in total, K2 (6, 0, 3, 7, 0, 4, 7), turn. 128 (136, 144, 150, 158, 166, 174, 180) sts. Place rem sts on a holder for Front.
Next row (WS): P2 (6, 0, 3, 7, 0, 4, 7), work from Chart row 2 as before (all sts purled), P3 (7, 0, 3, 7, 1, 5, 8).
Continue to work from chart with st st at edges where appropriate, until 72 (72, 76, 76, 82, 82, 86, 86) rows of patt are complete (a few extra rows are given on the chart, in case extra depth is required).

SHAPE SHOULDERS

Ensure that all casting off is done **very loosely** so that the top will block out to measurements correctly. If necessary use a significantly larger needle.
Now working in st st only, cast off 7 (7, 8, 8, 9, 9, 10, 11) sts at start of next 2 rows. 114 (122, 128, 134, 140, 148, 154, 158) sts.
Cast off 7 (7, 8, 9, 9, 10, 10, 11) sts at start of next row, then knit until you have 27 (31, 32, 34, 36, 39, 41, 42) sts on needle after cast-off sts. Turn. Place rem 80 (84, 88, 91, 95, 99, 103, 105) sts on a holder for left shoulder and back neck.
Cast off 3 (3, 3, 3, 4, 4, 4, 4) sts at start of next row and purl to end.
Cast off 7 (8, 8, 9, 9, 10, 10, 11) sts at start of next row and knit to end. 17 (20, 21, 22, 23, 25, 27, 27) sts.
Cast off 4 (4, 4, 4, 5, 5, 5, 5) sts at start of next row and purl to end.
Cast off 7 (8, 8, 9, 9, 10, 11, 11) sts at start of next row and knit to end. 6 (8, 9, 9, 9, 10, 11, 11) sts.
Cast off rem sts.

Return to sts on holder and place centre 46 (46, 48, 48, 50, 50, 52, 52) sts on a holder for back neck.
With RS facing rejoin yarn at neck edge and knit to end of row. 34 (38, 40, 43, 45, 49, 51, 53) sts.
Cast off 7 (7, 8, 9, 9, 10, 10, 11) sts at start of next row and purl to end. 27

(31, 32, 34, 36, 39, 41, 42) sts.
Cast off 3 (3, 3, 3, 4, 4, 4, 4) sts at start
of next row and knit to end.
Cast off 7 (8, 8, 9, 9, 10, 10, 11) sts at
start of next row and purl to end. 17
(20, 21, 22, 23, 25, 27, 27) sts.
Cast off 4 (4, 4, 4, 5, 5, 5, 5) sts at start
of next row and knit to end.
Cast off 7 (8, 8, 9, 9, 10, 11, 11) sts at
start of next row and purl to end. 6 (8,
9, 9, 9, 10, 11, 11) sts.
Cast off rem sts.

Front

Return to 128 (136, 144, 150, 158, 166,
174, 180) sts on holder for Front.
With RS facing, rejoin yarn and work in
lace patt as foll:
Next row (RS): K3 (7, 0, 3, 7, 1, 5, 8),
work Chart row 1, repeating marked
section 5 (5, 6, 6, 6, 7, 7, 7) times in
total, K2 (6, 0, 3, 7, 0, 4, 7), turn.
Next row (WS): P2 (6, 0, 3, 7, 0, 4, 7),
work from Chart row 2 as before (all
sts purled), P3 (7, 0, 3, 7, 1, 5, 8).
Continue to work from chart with st st
at edges where appropriate, until 38
(38, 40, 40, 42, 42, 44, 44) rows of patt
are complete.
Keeping lace patt corr as set (and only
working motifs if you have enough sts
and rows to work the whole motif –
otherwise replace with st st), patt 51
(55, 58, 61, 64, 68, 71, 74) and place
rem 77 (81, 86, 89, 94, 98, 103, 106) sts
on holder for right shoulder and front
neck. Turn.
Keeping patt corr, cast off 3
(3, 3, 3, 4, 4, 4, 4) sts at start of next
and foll alt row. 45 (49, 52, 55, 56,
60, 63, 66) sts.
Keeping patt corr, dec 1 st at
neck edge on next 7 rows and then on
foll 4 alt rows. 34 (38, 41, 44, 45, 49,
52, 55) sts.
Work straight in patt until Front
matches Back to start of shoulder
shaping, ending with RS facing for
next row.

SHAPE SHOULDERS

Ensure that all casting off is done **very**
loosely so that the top will block out to
measurements correctly. If necessary
use a significantly larger needle.
Now working in st st only, cast off 7 (7,
8, 8, 9, 9, 10, 11) sts at start of next row.
27 (31, 33, 36, 36, 40, 42, 44) sts.
Work 1 row straight.
Cast off 7 (7, 8, 9, 9, 10, 10, 11) sts at
start of next row.

Key

- ☐ Knit on RS, Purl on WS
- ○ Yarnover
- ◣ SSK
- ⋏ Sl 1, K2tog, psso
- ☐ Pattern repeat

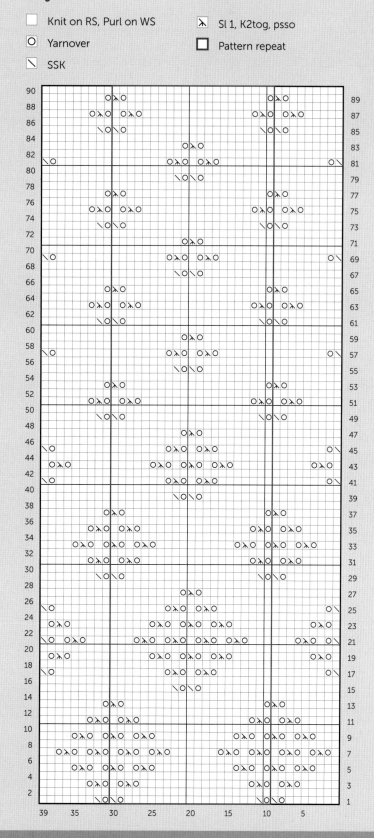

Tirrold continued

will keep the edges straight. Fully stretch out the rib welts. Leave until completely dry.
Join shoulder seams.

ARMHOLE EDGING
With RS facing, starting at underarm marker and using 2.5mm circular needles (or DPNs if preferred), pick up and knit 120 (120, 128, 128, 136, 136, 144, 144) sts around armhole edge.
Place marker for start of round.
Round 1: *K2, P2; rep from * to end of round.
This round sets rib. Repeat last round until rib measures 3cm.
Cast off very loosely in rib.

Repeat for other armhole.

NECK EDGING
Starting at left shoulder seam, with RS facing and using 2.5mm circular needles, pick up and knit 20 (20, 22, 22, 24, 24, 26, 26) sts down left neck edge to start of curve, pick up and knit 28 (28, 28, 28, 30, 30, 30, 30) sts along curved edge, knit 26 (26, 28, 28, 30, 30, 32, 32) sts from front neck holder, pick up and knit 28 (28, 28, 28, 30, 30, 30, 30) sts from right neck curve and pick up and knit 20 (20, 22, 22, 24, 24, 26, 26) sts up to right shoulder seam, pick up and knit 8 (8, 8, 8, 10, 10, 10, 10) sts down back neck, knit 46 (46, 48, 48, 50, 50, 52, 52) sts from back neck holder, pick up and knit 8 (8, 8, 8, 10, 10, 10, 10) sts from left shoulder. 184 (184, 192, 192, 208, 208, 216, 216) sts.
Work in rib, as for armhole edging, until rib measures 3cm.
Cast off very loosely.
Weave in all ends. If necessary, repeat the blocking procedure to open out the rib at neck and armholes.

Work 1 row straight.
Cast off 7 (8, 8, 9, 9, 10, 10, 11) sts at start of next row.
Work 1 row straight.
Cast off 7 (8, 8, 9, 9, 10, 10, 11) sts at start of next row. 6 (8, 9, 9, 10, 11, 11) sts.
Cast off rem sts.

Return to 77 (81, 86, 89, 94, 98, 103, 106) sts on holder and place centre 26 (26, 28, 28, 30, 30, 32, 32) sts on a holder for Front neck. With RS facing, rejoin yarn at neck edge of rem 51 (55, 58, 61, 64, 68, 71, 74) sts.
Keeping lace patt corr as before, cast off 3 (3, 3, 3, 4, 4, 4, 4) sts at start of next and foll alt rows (both will be RS) and patt to end. 45 (49, 52, 55, 56, 60, 63, 66) sts.
Keeping patt corr, work 1 row straight, and then dec 1 st at neck edge on next 7 rows and then on foll 4 alt rows. 34 (38, 41, 44, 45, 49, 52, 55) sts.
Work straight in patt until Front matches Back to start of shoulder shaping, ending with WS facing for next row.
Ensure that all casting off is done very loosely so that the top will block out to measurements correctly. If necessary use a significantly larger needle.
Now working in st st only, work shoulder shaping to match first side.

Making up
Soak garment in tepid water for 20 minutes. Squeeze gently and place between towels. Press to remove excess water. Block top by pinning out to measurements, stretching firmly. Blocking wires may be useful as they

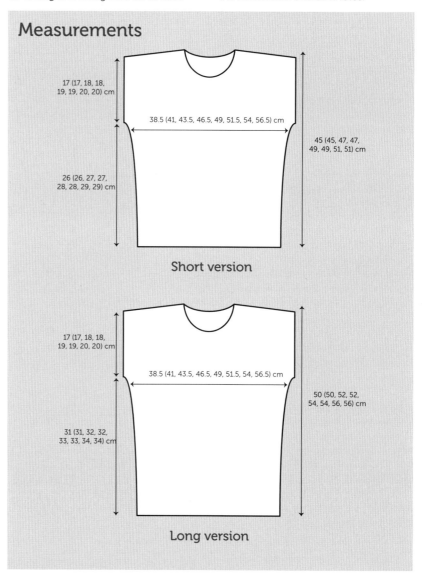

Measurements

17 (17, 18, 18, 19, 19, 20, 20) cm

38.5 (41, 43.5, 46.5, 49, 51.5, 54, 56.5) cm

45 (45, 47, 47, 49, 49, 51, 51) cm

26 (26, 27, 27, 28, 28, 29, 29) cm

Short version

17 (17, 18, 18, 19, 19, 20, 20) cm

38.5 (41, 43.5, 46.5, 49, 51.5, 54, 56.5) cm

50 (50, 52, 52, 54, 54, 56, 56) cm

31 (31, 32, 32, 33, 33, 34, 34) cm

Long version

Hethe

by Judy Furlong

A feminine cardigan with exquisite lace detailing.

Pattern notes

Cast on fairly loosely, to allow the lace pattern to be stretched out during blocking.

The Front decreases are worked on every second cable row after the section in single rib.

The Body is knitted in one section to the armholes after which it is divided into Back, Left Front and Right Front. The lace for the cuff and front edge are knitted separately and sewn on later and so may be omitted if preferred.

Skills

Complex lace, cables, knitted-on edging, working from charts

Size

To fit bust

6	8-10	12-14	16-18	20-22	24-26	
76	81-86	91-96	101-106	111-118	121-128	cm
30	31-34	36-38	40-42	44-46	48-50	in

Actual bust

86	96	106	115	128	138	cm
34	38	42	45	50	54	in

Actual back length, including lace

51	52	53	54	55	56	cm
20	20½	21	21¼	21½	22	in

Sleeve seam

29cm, 11½in all sizes

Yarn

Fyberspates Scrumptious Lace (45% silk, 55% merino; 100g skeins)
Rose Pink (509) 1 (2, 2, 2, 3, 3) x 100g skeins
Note: Smallest size uses approx 94g, so depending on swatch size and tension, 2 skeins may be required.

Needles and accessories

1 pair 3mm (UK 11/US 2-3) knitting needles
1 pair 2.75mm (UK 12/US 2) (UK 12/US 2) knitting needles
Cable needle (cn)
Stitch markers, stitch holders, row markers
2 x buttons, approx 15mm

Tension

25 sts and 38 rows to 10cm using 3mm needles over st st
31 sts and 38 rows to 10cm using 3mm needles over lace patt, after blocking

Special abbreviations

C6B Slip 3 sts to cn and hold at back, K3; K3 from cn
MB Make a bobble. [P1, K1, P1] all into next stitch, turn. K1, P1, K1, turn. K1, P1, K1, slip sts 1 and 2 over stitch 3.
Nupp7 [(K1, yo) 3 times, K1] all into next stitch to make 7 sts from 1. On the next row, purl all 7 loops together.
P7tog Purl 7 sts together to complete the nupp.
sk2po Slip one stitch knitwise, K2tog, pass slipped stitch over
w&t Wrap and turn. Take yarn to opposite side of work (between the needles), slip next stitch purlwise from LH to RH needle, return yarn to original side of work, return slipped stitch to LH needle without twisting. The stitch is now wrapped with yarn. Turn work and start next row leaving any remaining sts unworked. When this stitch is eventually worked, knit (or purl) the wrap and the stitch together as one stitch.

Standard abbreviations appear on page 71.

Body

PEPLUM

With 3mm needles, cast on 225 (249, 285, 309, 345, 381) sts.
The following section is also shown on the Chart, which appears on page 33.

Row 1 (WS): P1, K1, P2, K1, *P5, MB, P5, K1; rep from * to last 4 sts, P2, K1, P1.

Row 2 (RS): K1, P1, [K1, yo, K1] all into next st, [K1, yo, K1] all into next st, P1, *Nupp7, yo, K3, sk2po, K3, yo, Nupp7, P1; rep from * to the last 4 sts, [K1, yo, K1] all into next st, [K1, yo, K1] all into next st, P1, K1. 233 (257, 293, 317, 353, 389) sts (counting each nupp as 1 st, rather than 7).

Row 3: P1, K1, P6, K1, *P7tog to finish nupp, P9, P7tog to finish nupp, K1; rep from * until 8 sts remain, P6, K1, P1. Cont to foll chart from Row 4, until Row 29 has been completed.

WAISTBAND

Change to 2.75mm needles and work in patt as foll:

Row 1 (RS): K1, P1, K6, P1, *[K1, P1] twice, sk2po, P1, [K1, P1] twice; rep from * to last 8 sts, K6, P1, K1. 197 (217, 247, 267, 297, 327) sts.

Rows 2, 4, 6 & 8: P1, K1, P6, K1, *P1, K1; rep from * to last 8 sts, P6, K1, P1.

Row 3 (buttonhole): K1, P1, C6B, yo, K2tog, P1, *K1, P1; rep from * to last 8 sts, C6B, P1, K1.

Row 5: K1, P1, K6, P1, *K1, P1; rep from * to last 8 sts, K6, P1, K1.

Row 7: K1, P1, C6B, P1, *K1, P1; rep from * to last 8 sts, C6B, P1, K1.

Rows 9 to 16: Rep last 4 rows 2 times.
Rows 17 & 18: Rep Rows 5 & 6.
Rows 19 & 20: Rep Rows 3 & 4.

MAIN SECTION

Change to 3mm needles and work in st st with cable borders as foll:

Row 1 (RS): K1, P1, K6, P1, K30 (15, 114, 24, 19, 154), [M1, K59 (28, 0, 50, 40, 0)] 2 (6, 0, 4, 6, 0) times, M1, K31 (16, 115, 25, 20, 155) sts, P1, K6, P1, K1. 200 (224, 248, 272, 304, 328) sts.

Hethe continued

Row 2 (place side markers): P1, K1, P6, K1, P46 (52, 58, 64, 72, 78), pm, P90 (102, 114, 126, 142, 154), pm, P46 (52, 58, 64, 72, 78) K1, P6, K1, P1.
In the next row you will place markers for the darts (it is advisable to use a different type or colour of marker to avoid confusion).

Row 3 (place dart markers): K1, P1, C6B, P1, K16 (18, 20, 22, 25, 27), pm, K30 (34, 38, 42, 47, 51), slm, K30 (34, 38, 42, 47, 51), pm, K30 (34, 38, 42, 48, 52), pm, K30 (34, 38, 42, 47, 51), slm, K30 (34, 38, 42, 47, 51), pm, K16 (18, 20, 22, 25, 27), P1, C6B, P1, K1.

Row 4: P1, K1, P6, K1, purl to last 9 sts slipping markers, K1, P6, K1, P1.

Row 5: K1, P1, K6, P1, knit to last 9 sts, slipping markers, P1, K6, P1, K1.

Row 6: As Row 4.

Row 7 (1st Front dec): K1, P1, C6B, P1, SSK, knit to last 11 sts, slipping markers, K2tog, P1, C6B, P1, K1. 198 (222, 246, 270, 302, 326) sts.

Row 8: As Row 4.
Continue in st st with 9 st cable borders as set and with Front decreases on Row 15 and the 15 (17, 17, 18, 19, 19) foll 8th rows, 17 (19, 19, 20, 21, 21) front decs in total, and **at the same time**, work Side, Back and Front shaping as foll:

Row 11: K1, P1, C6B, P1, knit to 1st side marker (**right Side**), slm, K1, M1, knit to 1 st before 2nd side marker (**left Side**), M1, K1, slm, knit to last 9 sts, P1, C6B, P1, K1. 200 (224, 248, 272, 304, 328) sts.

Rows 12 to 18: As est remembering Front decs on Row 15. 198 (222, 246, 270, 302, 326) sts.

Row 19: K1, P1, C6B, P1, knit to 1 st before 1st front dart marker (**right Front**), M1, K1, slm, K1, M1, knit to 1 st before 2nd front dart marker (**left Front**), slipping side and back dart markers, M1, K1, slm, K1, M1, knit to last 9 sts, P1, C6B, P1, K1. 202 (226, 250, 274, 306, 330) sts.

Rows 20 to 22: As est.

Row 23: K1, P1, C6B, P1, SSK, knit to 1 st before 1st back dart marker, slipping front dart and side markers, M1, K1, slm, K1, M1, knit to 1 st before 2nd back dart marker, M1, K1, slm, K1, M1, knit to last 11 sts, K2tog, P1, C6B, P1, K1. 204 (228, 252, 276, 308, 332) sts.

Rows 24 to 38: As est remembering Front decs on Row 31. 202 (226, 250, 274, 306, 330) sts.

Row 39: K1, P1, C6B, P1, SSK, knit to 1 st before 1st front dart marker (**right Front**), M1, K1, slm, K1, M1, knit to 1 st before 1st side marker (**right Side**), M1, K1, slm, K1, M1, knit to 1 st before 2nd side marker (**left Side**) slipping back dart markers, M1, K1, slm, K1, M1, knit to 1 st before 2nd front dart marker (**left Front**), M1, K1, slm, K1, M1, knit to last 11 sts, K2tog, P1, C6B, P1, K1. 208 (232, 256, 280, 312, 336) sts.

Rows 40 to 44: As est.

Row 45: K1, P1, K6, P1, knit to 1 st before 1st back dart marker, slipping front dart and side markers, M1, K1, slm, K1, M1, knit to 1 st before 2nd back dart marker, M1, K1, slm, K1, M1, knit to last 9 sts, P1, K6, P1, K1. 212 (236, 260, 284, 316, 340) sts.

Rows 46 to 58: As est remembering Front decs on Rows 47 and 55. 208 (232, 256, 280, 312, 336) sts.

Row 59: K1, P1, C6B, P1, knit to 1 st before 1st front dart marker (**right Front**), M1, K1, slm, K1, M1, knit to to 1 st before 2nd front dart marker (**left Front**), M1, K1, slm, K1, M1, knit to last 9 sts, P1, C6B, P1, K1. 212 (236, 260, 284, 316, 340) sts.

Rows 60 to 66: As est remembering Front decs on Row 63. 210 (234, 258, 282, 314, 338) sts.

Row 67: K1, P1, C6B, P1, knit to 1 st before 1st side marker (**right Side**), M1, K1, slm, K1, M1, knit to 1 st before 1st back dart marker, M1, K1, slm, K1, M1, knit to 1 st before 2nd back dart marker, M1, K1, slm, K1, M1, knit to 1 st before 2nd side marker (**left Side**), M1, K1, slm, K1, M1, knit to last 9 sts, P1, C6B, P1, K1. 218 (242, 256, 290, 322, 346) sts.

Row 68: Patt to end.

In the following two sections (right and left front bust darts), the row numbering is given for pairs of short rows, and repeats when you work the left front. This is because the rows are not worked across the whole length of the row, and thus on the second side you are in effect working the other ends of the same set of rows.

RIGHT FRONT BUST DART

Short Row 69 (RS, bust dart): Patt to 12 (13, 15, 16, 18, 19) sts before 1st side marker, w&t, patt to end (**right Front edge**).

Short Row 71 (RS): Remembering Front dec, patt to 24 (26, 30, 32, 36, 38) sts before 1st side marker, w&t, patt to end (**right Front edge**).

Short Row 73 (RS): Patt to Front dart, *35 (39, 43, 47, 52, 56) sts before 1st side marker*, w&t, patt to end.

Short Row 75 (RS): Patt to 29 (32, 35, 40, 44, 47) sts before 1st side marker, w&t, patt to end.

Short Row 77 (RS): Patt to 18 (19, 21, 25, 27, 29) sts before 1st side marker, w&t, patt to end.

Short Row 79 (RS): Remembering Front dec, patt to 6 (6, 7, 9, 10, 11) sts before 1st side marker, w&t, patt to end.

Row 81 (RS): Patt to end (**to left Front edge**).

LEFT FRONT BUST DART

Short Row 70 (WS): Patt to 12 (13, 15, 16, 18, 19) sts before 1st side marker, w&t, patt to end remembering Front dec (**left Front edge**).

Short Row 72 (WS): Patt to 24 (26, 30, 32, 36, 38) sts before 1st side marker, w&t, patt to end (**left Front edge**).

Short Row 74 (WS): Patt to Front dart, *35 (39, 43, 47, 52, 56) sts before 1st side marker*, w&t, patt to end.

Short Row 76 (WS): Patt to 29 (32, 35, 40, 44, 47) sts before 1st side marker, w&t, patt to end.

Short Row 78 (WS): Patt to 18 (19, 21, 25, 27, 29) sts before 1st side marker, w&t, patt to end remembering Front dec.

Short Row 80 (WS): Patt to 6 (6, 7, 9, 10, 11) sts before 1st side marker, w&t, patt to end.

Row 82 (WS): Patt to end (**to right Front edge**).

Rows 83 to 88: Cont in patt as est, remembering Front dec on Row 87, removing Front and Back dart markers but leaving both side markers. 212 (236, 250, 284, 316, 340) sts.

Divide Fronts and Back

Divide for Fronts and Back and shape armholes as follows:

Row 1 (RS): Patt to 1st side marker, remove marker, slip these 52 (58, 64, 70, 78, 84) sts onto a stitch holder and set aside for Right Front. Cast off 4 (4, 5, 6, 7, 8) sts, knit to 2nd marker, slip remaining 52 (58, 64, 70, 78, 84) sts on stitch holder and set aside for Left Front. Turn. Continue on these 104 (116, 127, 138, 153, 164) sts only for Back.

Back

Row 2 (WS): Cast off 4 (4, 5, 6, 7, 8) sts purlwise, purl to end. 100 (112, 122, 132, 146, 156) sts.
Row 3: K1, K2tog, knit to last 3 sts, SSK, K1.
Row 4: P1, P2tog tbl, purl to last 3 sts, P2tog, P1.
Repeat last 2 rows 1 (1, 2, 2, 4, 5) more times. 92 (104, 110, 120, 126, 132) sts.
Next row: As Row 3.
Next row: Purl.
Rep last 2 rows 5 (7, 8, 10, 11, 13) more times. 80 (88, 92, 98, 102, 104) sts.
Work in st st without further shaping for 22 (22, 22, 22, 20, 18) rows.
Next row: K1, M1, knit to last st, M1, K1.
Work in st st for 5 rows.
Repeat last 6 rows, 4 more times. 90 (98, 102, 108, 112, 114) sts.

RIGHT SHOULDER

Row 1 (RS): Cast off 10 (10, 11, 12, 12, 12) sts, knit to 20 (22, 23, 24, 25, 26) sts on right needle, SSK, turn. Work on these 21 (23, 24, 25, 26, 27) sts only for Right shoulder.
Row 2: P2tog tbl, purl to end.
Row 3: Cast off 9 (10, 11, 11, 12, 12) sts, knit to last 2 sts, SSK, turn.
Row 4: As Row 2.
Cast off rem 9 (10, 10, 11, 11, 12) sts.

BACK NECK AND LEFT SHOULDER

With RS facing, slip centre 26 (30, 30, 32, 34, 34) sts onto waste yarn for Back neck.
Row 1 (RS): Rejoin yarn to Left shoulder sts, K2tog, knit to end. 31 (33, 35, 37, 38, 39) sts.
Row 2: Cast off 10 (10, 11, 12, 12, 12) sts, purlwise, purl to last 2 sts, P2tog. Complete to match first side, reversing shapings.

Measurements

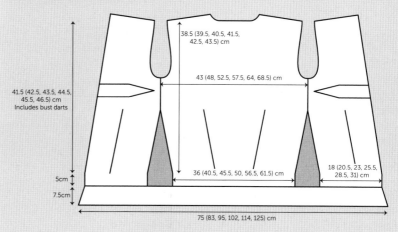

38.5 (39.5, 40.5, 41.5, 42.5, 43.5) cm

43 (48, 52.5, 57.5, 64, 68.5) cm

41.5 (42.5, 43.5, 44.5, 45.5, 46.5) cm
Includes bust darts

36 (40.5, 45.5, 50, 56.5, 61.5) cm

18 (20.5, 23, 25.5, 28.5, 31) cm

5cm

7.5cm

75 (83, 95, 102, 114, 125) cm

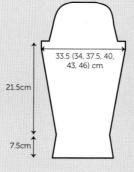

33.5 (34, 37.5, 40, 43, 46) cm

21.5cm

7.5cm

Key

☐	Knit on RS, Purl on WS
●	Purl on RS, Knit on WS
◣	Sl 1, K1, psso on RS, P2tog tbl on WS
◢	K2tog on RS, P2tog on WS
⋊	Sl 1, K2tog, psso
⋀	K7tog on RS, P7tog on WS
O	Yarnover
♉	Nupp7
⋎	[K1, yo, K1] all into same stitch
B	MB
▨	C6B
▨	No stitch, ignore these squares and move straight to next knitting instruction
☐	Pattern repeat

Chart

Wrong side rows are read from left to right and right side rows are read from right to left. The repeat section is marked on the chart by a red box.

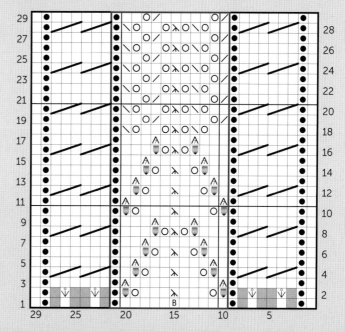

Left Front

SHAPE ARMHOLE

With RS facing, rejoin yarn at left armhole to 52 (58, 64, 70, 78, 84) sts and remembering **at the same time** to work Front decs (11 decs have been worked to this point, 6 (8, 8, 9, 10, 10) decs remain *the next dec falls on Row 3*), shape armhole as foll:

Row 1 (RS): Cast off 4 (4, 5, 6, 7, 8) sts, patt to end. 48 (54, 59, 64, 71, 76) sts.
Row 2: Patt to end.
Row 3: K1, K2tog, patt to end.
Row 4: Patt to last 3 sts, P2tog, P1.
Rep last 2 rows 1 (1, 2, 2, 4, 5) more times.
Next row: As Row 3.
Next row: Purl.
Rep last 2 rows 5 (7, 8, 10, 11, 13) more times.
Work in st st without further armhole shaping (*Front decs only*) for 22 (22, 22, 22, 20, 18) rows.
Next row (RS): K1, M1, patt to end.
Patt 5 rows.
Rep last 6 rows, 4 more times (thus completing Front decs). 37 (39, 41, 43, 44, 45) sts.

SHAPE SHOULDER

Row 1 (RS): Cast off 10 (10, 11, 12, 12, 12) sts, patt to end.
Row 2: Patt to end.
Row 3: Cast off 9 (10, 11, 11, 12, 12) sts, patt to end.
Row 4: As Row 2.
Cast off 8 (9, 9, 10, 10, 11) sts.** Slip rem 10 sts onto waste yarn.

Right Front

SHAPE ARMHOLE

Work as for Left Front, reversing shapings (work armhole and shoulder cast offs purlwise on WS rows), to **.

BACK NECK BAND

Continue on rem 10 sts as est, for a further 52 (56, 56, 60, 64, 64) rows. Slip these sts onto waste yarn.

Sleeves

Make 2 alike
CABLE BAND

Cast on 10 sts.
Row 1 (RS): K1, P1, K6, P1, K1.
Row 2: P1, K1, P6, K1, P1.
Row 3: K1, P1, C6B, P1, K1.
Row 4: As Row 2.
Repeat the last 4 rows 24 (27, 28, 29, 30, 31) more times. Cast off.

MAIN SECTION

With RS facing, pick up and knit 64 (72, 74, 76, 78, 80) sts from edge of band. Then, starting with a purl row, work 5 (7, 3, 1, 1, 1) rows in st st.
Next row (RS): K1, M1, knit to last st, M1, K1.
Work in st st for 6 (10, 6, 5, 4, 3) more rows.
Cont as est, inc 1 st at both ends of the next row and 8 (5, 8, 10, 13, 16) following 7th (11th, 7th, 6th, 5th, 4th) rows. 84 (86, 94, 100, 108, 116) sts.
Work in st st, without shaping, for a further 12 (7, 14, 13, 9, 11) rows, ending with RS facing for next row.

SHAPE SLEEVEHEAD

Rows 1 & 2: Cast off 5 (5, 6, 7, 8, 9) sts at beginning of next 2 rows. 74 (76, 82, 86, 92, 98) sts.
Row 3: K1, K2tog, knit to last 3 sts, SSK, K1.
Row 4: P1, P2tog tbl, purl to last 3 sts, P2tog, P1.
Rep last 2 rows 1 (1, 2, 2, 4, 5) more times. 66 (68, 70, 74, 72,74) sts.
Next row: As Row 3.
Next row: Purl.
Rep last 2 rows 5 (7, 8, 10, 11, 13) more times.
54 (52, 52, 52, 48, 46) sts.
Work without further shaping for 0 (0, 0, 2, 6, 6) rows.
Next row: As Row 3.
Work in st st for 3 rows.
Repeat last 4 rows 3 (3, 3, 2, 1, 1) more times. 46 (44, 44, 46, 44, 42) sts.
Next row: As Row 3.
Next row: Purl.
Rep last 2 rows 7 (5, 4, 4, 3, 2) more times. 30 (32, 34, 36, 36, 36) sts.
Next row: As Row 3.
Next row: As Row 4. 26 (28, 30, 32, 32, 32) sts.
Cast off 3 (3, 4, 4, 4, 4) sts at beginning of next 2 rows.
Cast off 5 (6, 6, 7, 7, 7) sts at beginning of next 2 rows.
Cast off rem 10 sts.

FRONT LACE

With 3mm needles, loosely cast on 457 (469, 469, 481, 493, 505) sts.
Row 1 (WS): *K1, P5, MB, P5; rep from * to last st, K1. 38 (39, 39, 40, 41, 42) patt repeats in all.
Row 2: P1, *Nupp7, yo, K3, sk2po, K3, yo, Nupp7, P1; rep from * to end.

Row 3: *K1, P7tog to finish nupp, P9, P7tog to finish nupp; rep from * to last st, K1.
Continue following chart, sts 9 to 21 only (*omitting cable edge sts 1-8 and 22-29*), until Row 17 has been completed.
Cast off loosely.

CUFF LACE

With 3mm needles, loosely cast on 73 (85, 97, 97, 97, 97) sts.
Row 1 (WS): *K1, P5, MB, P5; rep from * to last st, K1. 6 (7, 8, 8, 8, 8) patt repeats in all.
Row 2: P1, *Nupp7, yo, K3, sk2po, K3, yo, Nupp7, P1; rep from * to end.
Row 3: *K1, P7tog to finish nupp, P9, P7tog to finish nupp; rep from * to last st, K1.
Continue following chart, sts 9 to 21 only (*omitting cable edge sts 1-8 and 22-29*), until Row 22 has been completed.
Row 23: K1, *P2, yo, P2tog, P3tog, P2, yo, P2tog, K1; rep from * to end. 61 (71, 81, 81, 81, 81) sts.
Cast off very loosely.

Making up

Block cardigan to measurements. When blocking this garment, soak fully in tepid water for at least 20 minutes, then squeeze out excess water and pin out to measurements, stretching firmly if needed. Blocking wires may be useful as they will keep the edges straight. Take care **not** to stretch waist ribbing or to flatten out bust dart.

Once dry, join shoulder seams. Graft ends of left and right cable borders together using Kitchener stitch (or use the 3-needle cast-off method). Sew edge of cable border to Back Neck. Sew cast-off edge of Front Lace to free edge of cable border (approx 1 cast-off st to every row). Attach Cuff Lace to free edge of Cuff Cable Border. Join underarm seam from edge of lace. Fit sleeves into armholes. Gently press or steam all seams open. Sew on buttons to match buttonholes.

Childry

by Elly Doyle

A gently ruffled edge softens this traditionally shaped small shawl.

Pattern notes

A simple but very effective garter stitch triangular shawl, knitted from the top down. Starts with a short cast on and increases evenly on both sides of a central spine, in the Faroese tradition.

Shawl

Using the backwards loop cast-on method, for a stretchy edge, cast on 11 sts.

Row 1 (WS): K3, pm, K1, pm, K3, pm, K1, pm, K3.

Row 2 (RS): K3, slm, yo, K1, yo, slm, K3, slm, yo, K1, yo, slm, K3. 15 sts.

Row 3: Knit.

Row 4: K3, slm, yo, K3, yo, slm, K3, slm, yo, K3, yo, slm, K3. 19 sts.

Row 5: Knit.

Row 6: K3, slm, yo, knit to marker, yo, slm, K3, slm, yo, knit to marker, yo, slm, K3. 23 sts.

Row 7: Knit.

Last 2 rows set pattern. Work these two rows 50 more times, ending with RS facing for next row. 223 sts.

Row 108 (RS): *(K1, yo, K1) into the same st; rep from * into every st in the row. 669 sts.

Rows 109-114: Knit.

Next row (WS): Cast off all sts loosely.

Finishing

Weave in ends, but do not trim. Soak shawl in tepid water for 20 minutes. Squeeze gently and place between towels. Press to remove excess water. Lay a large towel on a flat surface, into which you can pin (carpet or foam tiles work well). Spread out the shawl to measurements and pin out to dry. When completely dry, unpin and trim ends.

Skills

Simple garter stitch, increasing and decreasing

Size

Wingspan approx 107cm (42in), relaxed after blocking
Nape of neck to bottom edge approx 48cm (19in)

Yarn

Fyberspates Scrumptious 4ply/Sport (45% silk, 55% superwash merino; 100g skeins)
Gold (302) 1 x 100g skein

Needles and accessories

1 pair 3.75mm (UK 9/US 5) knitting needles (you may find it easier to use a set of circular needles 80cm long, due to the number of stitches)
Stitch markers

Tension

19 sts and 32 rows to 10cm over garter stitch, relaxed after washing and blocking

Abbreviations

Standard abbreviations appear on page 71.

Measurements

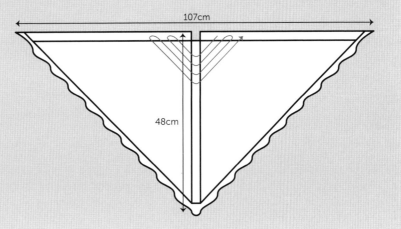

107cm

48cm

Arncott

by Jen Arnall-Culliford

A sassy, stylish hat to suit everyone, with a striking cabled diamond pattern.

Pattern notes

This cabled hat is knitted in the round on either double-pointed needles, or circular needles. The cables continue seamlessly around the hat.

Hat

Cast on 120 sts and join to work in the round, taking care not to twist stitches. Place marker for start of round.

Round 1: *K2, [P1, K1] 5 times, P1, K2; rep from * to end of round.
Last round sets rib. Work in rib until piece meas 3cm from cast-on edge. Now work 60 rounds in pattern by using either written instructions or the Chart.
Round 1: *T3F, [K1, P1] 4 times, K1, T3B; rep from * to end of round.
Round 2: *P1, K3, [P1, K1] 3 times, P1, K3, P1; rep from * to end of round.
Round 3: *P1, T3F, [P1, K1] 3 times, P1, T3B, P1; rep from * to end of round.
Round 4: *P2, K2, [P1, K1] 3 times, P1, K2, P2; rep from * to end of round.
Round 5: *P2, T3F, [K1, P1] twice, K1, T3B, P2; rep from * to end of round.
Round 6: *P3, K3, P1, K1, P1, K3, P3; rep from * to end of round.
Round 7: *P3, T3F, P1, K1, P1, T3B, P3; rep from * to end of round.
Round 8: *P4, K2, P1, K1, P1, K2, P4; rep from * to end of round.
Round 9: *P4, T3F, K1, T3B, P4; rep from * to end of round.
Round 10: *P5, K5, P5; rep from * to end of round.
Round 11: *P5, Tw5B, P5; rep from * to end of round.
Round 12: *P5, K2, P1, K2, P5; rep from * to end of round.
Round 13: *P4, T3B, K1, T3F, P4; rep from * to end of round.
Round 14: *P4, K3, P1, K3, P4; rep from * to end of round.
Round 15: *P3, C3B, P1, K1, P1, C3F, P3; rep from * to end of round.
Round 16: *P3, K2, [P1, K1] twice, P1, K2, P3; rep from * to end of round.
Round 17: *P2, T3B, [K1, P1] twice, K1, T3F, P2; rep from * to end of round.
Round 18: *P2, K3, [P1, K1] twice, P1, K3, P2; rep from * to end of round.
Round 19: *P1, C3B, [P1, K1] 3 times, P1, C3F, P1; rep from * to end of round.
Round 20: *P1, K2, [P1, K1] 4 times, P1, K2, P1; rep from * to end of round.
Round 21: *T3B, [K1, P1] 4 times, K1, T3F; rep from * to end of round.
Round 22: *K3, [P1, K1] 4 times, P1, K3; rep from * to last 15 sts, K3, [P1, K1] 4 times, P1, K1, slip next 2 sts to cn and remove start of round marker.
Round 23: Holding cn at front, K2, replace start of round marker, K2 from cn, *[P1, K1] 5 times, P1, C4F; rep from * to last 13 sts, [P1, K1] 5 times, P1, K2.
Round 24: *K3, [P1, K1] 4 times, P1, K3; rep from * to end of round.
Round 25: As Round 1.
Round 26: *P1, K2, [P1, K1] 4 times, P1, K2, P1; rep from * to end of round.
Round 27: As Round 3.
Round 28: *P2, K3, [P1, K1] twice, P1, K3, P2; rep from * to end of round.
Round 29: As Round 5.
Round 30: *P3, K2, [P1, K1] twice, P1, K2, P3; rep from * to end of round.
Round 31: As Round 7.
Round 32: *P4, K3, P1, K3, P4; rep from * to end of round.
Round 33: As Round 9.
Round 34: As Round 12.
Rounds 35-46: Work Rounds 11-22 once more.
Round 47: Holding sts on cn behind the main needle, knit together the first st on the cn with the first st on the main needle, replace start of round marker, then knit together the second st on each needle, *[P1, K1] 5 times, P1, C4to2; rep from * to last 12 sts, *[P1, K1] 6 times. 104 sts.
Round 48: *K2, [P1, K1] 4 times, P1, K2; rep from * to end of round.
Round 49: *SSK, [K1, P1] 4 times, K1, K2tog; rep from * to end of round. 88 sts.
Round 50: *[K1, P1] 5 times, K1; rep from * to end of round.

Skills

Cables and working in the round

Size

To fit average adult head
Circumference 50-55cm (19½-21½in)

Yarn

Fyberspates Scrumptious 4ply/Sport (45% silk, 55% superwash merino; 100g skeins)
Cherry (301) 1 x 100g skein

Needles and accessories

1 set 3.75mm (UK 9/US 5) double-pointed needles (or your preferred needles for knitting small diameters in the round)
2 cable needles (cn)
Stitch markers

Tension

1 cabled diamond meas 5.5cm by 6.5cm
27 sts and 38 rounds to 10cm over cable pattern after washing and blocking

Special abbreviations

See facing page.
Standard abbreviations appear on page 71.

Round 51: *SSK, [P1, K1] 3 times, P1, K2tog; rep from * to end of round. 72 sts.

Round 52: *K2, [P1, K1] twice, P1, K2; rep from * to end of round.

Round 53: *SSK, [K1, P1] twice, K1, K2tog; rep from * to end of round. 56 sts.

Round 54: *[K1, P1] 3 times, K1; rep from * to end of round.

Round 55: *SSK, P1, K1, P1, K2tog; rep from * to end of round. 40 sts.

Round 56: *K2, P1, K2; rep from * to end of round.

Round 57: *SSK, K1, K2tog; rep from * to end of round. 24 sts.

Round 58: *K1, P1, K1; rep from * to end of round.

Round 59: *K1, K2tog; rep from * to end of round. 16 sts.

Round 60: [K2tog] 8 times. 8 sts. Break yarn, pass through remaining sts and fasten off securely.

Finishing

Weave in all ends. Soak hat in tepid water for 20 minutes. Squeeze gently and place between towels. Press to remove excess water and block gently over a pudding basin.

Key

☐	Knit on RS
☐•	Purl on RS
◿	SSK on RS
◺	K2tog on RS
	T3B
	T3F
	C3B
	C3F
	Tw5B
	C4F
▨	Slip next 2 sts to cn
	Complete C4F using 2 sts on cn
	Complete C4to2 using 2 sts on cn
	C4to2

Special abbreviations

C3B: Slip 1 st to cn and hold at back, K2; K1 from cn

C3F: Slip 2 sts to cn and hold at front, K1; K2 from cn

C4F: Slip 2 sts to cn and hold at front, K2; K2 from cn

T3F: Slip 2 sts to cn and hold at front, P1; K2 from cn

T3B: Slip 1 st to cn and hold at back, K2; P1 from cn

Tw5B: Slip next 2 sts to first cn, slip next st to second cable needle and hold both cns at back of work, K2; P1 from second cn; K2 from first cn

C4to2: Slip next 2 sts to cn and hold at back, knit together the first st on the cn with the first st on the main needle, then knit together the second sts on each needle in the same way. 2 sts decreased.

Chart

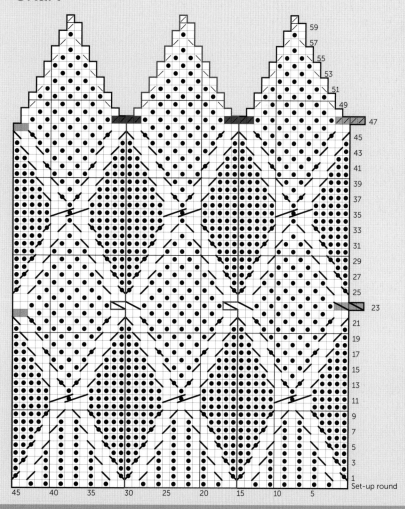

Challow
by Jeni Hewlett

Butterflies circle the yoke of this casual sweater.

Pattern notes
Challow is designed with 4cm
of negative ease. As knitwear is
inherently stretchy, this ensures
a snug fit. Choose the 'to fit' size
closest to your bust measurement.
Challow is knitted in the round, so
read all chart rows from right to left.

Body
Using colour A, cast on 208 (222, 236,
252, 264, 278, 292, 306) sts, pm and
join to work in the round, taking care
not to twist stitches.
Round 1: *K1, P1; rep from * to end of
round.
This round sets 1x1 rib.
Rep this round until piece meas 2.5
(2.5, 2.5, 2.5, 3, 3, 3, 3) cm. (Approx 10
(10, 10, 10, 12, 12, 12, 12) rounds.)
Next round: Knit.
This round sets st st in the round. Cont
to work in st st until piece meas 38 (38,
39, 39, 40, 40, 41, 41) cm.
Work 1 more round as foll: K86 (93,
100, 106, 112, 119, 124, 131), pm, K18
(18, 18, 20, 20, 20, 22, 22), pm, K86 (93,
100, 106, 112, 119, 124, 131), pm, K18
(18, 18, 20, 20, 20, 22, 22).
Leave sts on a spare needle or stitch
holders, and place 2 sets of 18 (18, 18,
20, 20, 20, 22, 22) sts on waste yarn for
underarm.

Sleeves
Make 2 alike
Using Colour A, cast on 42 (42, 44,
44, 46, 46, 48, 48) sts and join to work
in the round, taking care not to twist
stitches. Place marker to mark start
of round.
Work 10 rounds in 1x1 rib as set
by Body.
Change to st st and knit 4 rounds.
Next round (inc): K1, M1, knit to last
st, M1, K1. 44 (44, 46, 46, 48, 48, 50,
50) sts.
Work inc as set by last round inc
1 st on 7 (13, 13, 15, 17, 19, 20, 21) foll
6th rounds. 58 (70, 72, 76, 82, 86, 90,
92) sts.
Now inc as set on every foll 8th round
to 80 (82, 86, 88, 92, 94, 98, 100) sts.

Cont without shaping until sleeve
meas 39 (39, 40, 40, 41, 41, 42, 42)cm.
Next round: K71 (73, 77, 78, 82, 84, 87,
89), and put the next 18 (18, 18, 20, 20,
20, 22, 22) stitches on waste yarn 9 (9,
9, 10, 10, 10, 11, 11) sts from each side
of marker).

Yoke
Join sleeves and body as follows: K62
(64, 68, 68, 72, 74, 76, 78) (from first
sleeve), K86 (93, 100, 106, 112, 119,
124, 131) across front of Body, K62 (64,
68, 68, 72, 74, 76, 78) (from second
sleeve), K86 (93, 100, 106, 112, 119,
124, 131) across back of Body, pm for
start of round. 296 (314, 336, 348, 368,
386, 400, 418) sts.
Next round: Knit to end and at the
same time, inc 4 (1, 0, 0, 7, 4, 5, 2) sts
and dec 0 (0, 6, 3, 0, 0, 0, 0) sts evenly
across round. 300 (315, 330, 345, 375,
390, 405, 420) sts.
Work 9 more rounds in st st.
Next round: *K15, pm; rep from * to
end of round.
Next 3 rounds: Work rows 1 to 3 of
chart, repeating 15 st motif 20 (21, 22,
23, 25, 26, 27, 28) times in each round.
Work 4 rounds in st st using Colour A
only.
Next 13 rounds: Work rows 8 to 20
from chart, repeating 15 st motif 20
(21, 22, 23, 25, 26, 27, 28) times in
each round.
Next round: Knit.
Next round: Knit to end of round, w&t.
Short row 1 (WS): P86 (93, 100, 106,
112, 119, 124, 131), w&t.
Short row 2: K86 (93, 100, 106, 112,
119, 124, 131).
Next round: Knit, working wraps with
sts when you reach them.
Work 1 more round in st st.
Next 3 rounds: Work rows 25 to 27
from chart, repeating 15 st motif 20
(21, 22, 23, 25, 26, 27, 28) times in
each round.
Next round: Using colour A only, knit
to end of round, w&t.
Short row 1 (WS): P86 (93, 100, 106,
112, 119, 124, 131), w&t.

Short row 2: K86 (93, 100, 106, 112, 119, 124, 131).

Next round: Knit, working wraps with sts when you reach them.

Work 2 more rounds in st st.

Next round (dec): *K3, K2tog; rep from * to end of round. 240 (252, 264, 276, 300, 312, 324, 336) sts.

Work 2 (2, 2, 2, 4, 4, 4, 4) more rounds in st st.

Next round: *K2, P2; rep from *to end of round.

Rep last round 3 more times.

Next round (dec): *K2, P2tog; rep from * to end of round. 180 (189, 198, 207, 225, 234, 243, 252) sts.

Next round: *K2, P1; rep from * to end of round.

Last round sets 2x1 rib. Work 3 (3, 3, 3, 5, 5, 5, 5) more rounds in 2x1 rib.

Next round (dec): *K2tog, P1; rep from * to end of round. 120 (126, 132, 138, 150, 156, 162, 168) sts.

Next round: *K1, P1; rep from * to end of round.

Rep last round 3 (3, 3, 3, 4, 4, 4, 4) more times.

Cast off all sts in rib.

Finishing

Graft together the underarm sts on each side using Kitchener stitch. Weave in all ends, closing any gaps at the edges of the grafting if needed. Do not trim ends.

Soak sweater in tepid water for 20 minutes. Squeeze gently and place between towels. Press to remove excess water. Lay a large towel on a flat surface, into which you can pin (carpet or foam tiles work well). Spread out the sweater to measurements and pin out to dry. When completely dry, unpin and trim ends.

Key

- ■ Colour A; Knit
- ▨ Colour B; Knit
- □ Pattern repeat

Chart

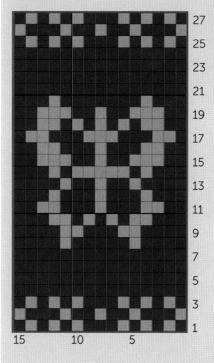

27
25
23
21
19
17
15
13
11
9
7
5
3
1

15   10   5

Special abbreviations

w&t: Wrap and turn. Take yarn to opposite side of work (between the needles), slip next stitch purlwise from LH to RH needle, return yarn to original side of work, return slipped stitch to LH needle without twisting. The stitch is now wrapped with yarn. Turn work and start next row leaving any remaining stitches unworked. When this stitch is eventually worked, knit (or purl) the wrap and the stitch together as one stitch.

Standard abbreviations appear on page 71.

Measurements

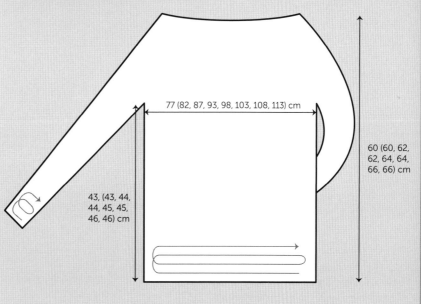

77 (82, 87, 93, 98, 103, 108, 113) cm

60 (60, 62, 62, 64, 64, 66, 66) cm

43, (43, 44, 44, 45, 45, 46, 46) cm

Skills
Shaping in lace

Sizes
To fit bust

8	10	12	14	16	18	20	22	
81	86	91	97	102	107	112	117	cm
32	34	36	38	40	42	44	46	in

Actual bust

84	89	94	100	105	110	115	120	cm
33	35	37	39¼	41¼	43¼	45¼	47¼	in

Actual length

51.5	53	54.5	56	57.5	59	60	60.5	cm
20	21	21½	22	22½	23	23½	23¾	in

Sleeve seam

47	48	48	49	50	50	50	50	cm
18½	18¾	18¾	19¼	19¾	19¾	19¾	19¾	in

Yarn
Fyberspates Scrumptious 4ply/Sport
(45% silk, 55% superwash merino;
100g skeins)
Teal (308) 3 (4, 4, 4, 4, 5, 5, 5) x
100g skeins

Needles and accessories
1 pair 3mm (UK 11/US 2-3) knitting needles
1 pair 3.5mm (UK 10-9/US 4) knitting
needles
1 set 3mm (UK 11/US 2-3) circular
needles, approx 100cm long
5 buttons, approx 1cm; Stitch holder
Spare yarn for marking corner sts on bands
3.25mm (US D-3) crochet hook for
button loops (optional as sewn button
loops can easily be made if you prefer)

Tension
20 sts and 34 rows to 10cm over lace
patt using 3.5mm needles, unstretched
25 sts and 32 rows to 10cm over mock
cable using 3.5mm needles

Stonor
by Belinda Boaden

A flattering cardigan for summer evenings.

Pattern notes
As this pattern has groups of sizes,
it is well worth reading through the
pattern carefully to start with and
circling your size throughout.
The lace pattern used has a
changing stitch count – only check
your numbers after rows 3 or 4.
The backward loop method is used
to work the M1 increase row between
the lace patt and the mock cables.
Other methods of working a M1 can
also be used.

Stitch patterns
MOCK CABLE FORWARD
(worked over 8 sts and 8 rows)
Row 1 (RS): P1, K7.
Row 2: P7 wrapping yarn round needle
twice for each stitch, K1.
Row 3: P1, C7F.
Rows 4 & 6: P7, K1.
Rows 5 & 7: As Row 1.
Row 8: As Row 4.

MOCK CABLE BACKWARD
(worked over 8 sts and 8 rows)
Row 1 (RS): P1, K7.
Row 2: P7 wrapping yarn round needle
twice for each stitch, K1.
Row 3: P1, C7B.
Rows 4 & 6: P7, K1.
Rows 5 & 7: As Row 1.
Row 8: As Row 4.

Back
Cast on 94 (98, 106, 110, 114, 122, 126,
130) sts using 3mm needles.
Row 1 (RS): *K2, P2; rep from * to last
2 sts, K2.
Row 2: *P2, K2; rep from * to last 2
sts, P2.
These 2 rows set rib. Cont in rib until
piece meas 14 (14, 14, 15, 15, 15, 16,
16) cm, ending with WS facing for
next row.

Sizes 8 (16): *Rib 7 (9), work2tog, [Rib
8 (10), work2tog] 3 times, Rib 7 (9),
work2tog; rep from * once, ending last
rep Rib 7 (9). 85 (105) sts.
Size 10: *Rib 8, work2tog; rep from *
to last 8 sts, Rib 8. 89 sts.

Sizes 12 (14, 20, 22): Rib 8 (10, 10, 12),
*work2tog, Rib 9 (9, 11, 11); rep from *
to last 10 (12, 12, 14) sts, work2tog, Rib
8 (10, 10, 12). 97 (101, 117, 121) sts.
Size 18: [Rib 10, work2tog, Rib 11,
work2tog] twice, Rib 10, work2tog,
[Rib 10, work2tog, Rib 11, work2tog]
twice, Rib 10. 113 sts.

Change to 3.5mm needles and begin
lace patt as foll:
Row 1 (RS): K1, *yo, K3, yo, K1; rep
from * to end.
Rows 2 & 4: Purl.
Row 3: K2, Sl 1, K2tog, psso, *K3,
Sl 1, K2tog, psso; rep from * to last
2 sts, K2. 85 (89, 97, 101, 105, 113, 117,
121) sts.

Work straight in lace patt until Back
meas approx 32 (33, 34, 35, 36, 37,
37.5, 37.5) cm from cast-on edge,
ending with a 4th patt row.

SHAPE ARMHOLES
Keeping lace patt correct, work
armhole shaping as foll:
Sizes 8 (10, 12): Cast off 4 sts at the
beg of the next 2 rows, 3 sts on the foll
2 (2, 4) rows, 2 sts on the next 2 (4, 2)
rows and 1 st at the beg of the next 4
(2, 2) rows. 63 (65, 71) sts.
Sizes 14 (16, 18): Cast off 4 sts at the
beg of the next 2 (2, 4) rows, 3 sts on
the foll 2 rows, 2 sts on the next 4 (6,
4) rows and 1 st at the beg of the next
6 (4, 4) rows. 73 (75, 79) sts.
Sizes 20 (22): Cast off 5 sts at the beg
of the next 2 rows, 4 sts on the foll 2
(4) rows, 3 sts at the beg of the next
4 (2) rows, 2 sts on the foll 2 (4) rows
and 1 st at the beg of the next 4 (2)
rows. 79 (79) sts.

Work 1 more row. You should have the
WS facing for next row and be ready
to work a 4th row of patt. 63 (65, 71, 73,
75, 79, 79, 79) sts.

Work increases ready for Mock Cable
patt as foll:
Sizes 8 (10): P1, *M1, P2; rep from * to
end. 94 (97) sts.

Size 12: P7, *M1, P2; rep from * to last 4 sts, P4. 101 sts.

Size 14: P1, [M1, P2] 17 times, M1, P1, [M1, P2] 18 times, M1, P1. 110 sts.

Size 16: P1 *[M1, P2] 18 times, M1, P1; rep from * once. 113 sts.

Sizes 18 (20, 22): P3, *M1, P2; rep from * to end. 117 (117, 117) sts.

SET MOCK CABLE PATTERN
Sizes 8 (14)
Row 1: P3 (2), *K7, P2; rep from * to last st, P1 (0).

Row 2: K3 (2), *P7 wrapping yarn round needle twice for each st, K2; rep from * to last st, K1 (0).

Row 3: P3 (2), [C7B, P2] 5 (6) times, [C7F, P2] 5 (6) times, P1 (0).

Sizes 10 (16)
Row 1: *P1, K7; rep from * to last st, P1.

Row 2: *K1, P7 wrapping yarn round needle twice for each st; rep from * to last st, K1.

Row 3: [P1, C7B] 6 (7) times, [P1, C7F] 6 (7) times, P1.

Size 12 (18, 20, 22)
Row 1: K2, *P1, K7; rep from * to last 3 sts, P1, K2.

Row 2: P2, *K1, P7 wrapping yarn round needle twice for each st; rep from * to last 3 sts, K1, P2.

Row 3: K2, [P1, C7B] 6 (7, 7, 7) times, [P1, C7F] 6 (7, 7, 7) times, P1, K2.

All sizes
Rows 4 & 6: Work sts as they face you (knit the knits and purl the purls).

Rows 5 & 7: As Row 1.

Row 8: Work sts as they face you.
Rep rows 1-8 inclusive until Back meas 49.5 (51, 52.5, 54, 55.5, 57, 58, 58.5) cm from cast-on edge.

SHAPE SHOULDERS
Keeping patt correct, cast off 8 (8, 9, 9, 10, 10, 10, 10) sts at beg of the next 2 rows, 8 (8, 9, 10, 10, 10, 10, 10) on the foll 2 rows and 8 (9, 9, 10, 11, 11, 11, 11) sts on the next 2 rows. Place rem 46 (47, 47, 52, 51, 55, 55, 55) sts on a holder for back neck.

Left front
Cast on 43 (43, 47, 51, 51, 55, 59, 59) sts using 3mm needles.

Row 1 (RS): *K2, P2; rep from * to last 3 sts, K3.

Row 2: P3, *K2, P2; rep from * to end.
These 2 rows set rib. Cont to work in rib until piece meas 14 (14, 14, 15, 15,

Measurements

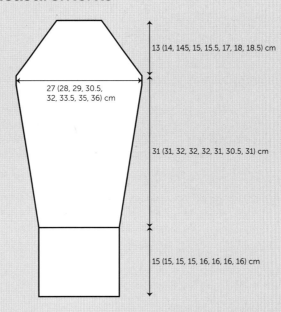

13 (14, 145, 15, 15.5, 17, 18, 18.5) cm

27 (28, 29, 30.5, 32, 33.5, 35, 36) cm

31 (31, 32, 32, 32, 31, 30.5, 31) cm

15 (15, 15, 15, 16, 16, 16, 16) cm

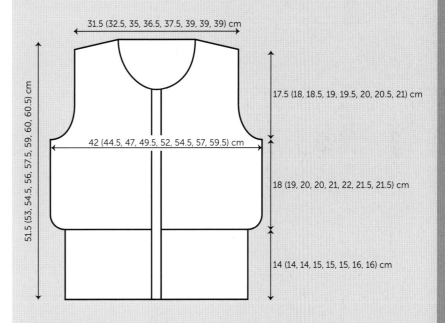

31.5 (32.5, 35, 36.5, 37.5, 39, 39, 39) cm

51.5 (53, 54.5, 56, 57.5, 59, 60, 60.5) cm

42 (44.5, 47, 49.5, 52, 54.5, 57, 59.5) cm

17.5 (18, 18.5, 19, 19.5, 20, 20.5, 21) cm

18 (19, 20, 20, 21, 22, 21.5, 21.5) cm

14 (14, 14, 15, 15, 15, 16, 16) cm

Special abbreviations

C7F: Slip next 7 sts from LH to RH needle p-wise, dropping extra loops made on the previous row, slip them back to LH needle passing the first 4 sts over the last 3 and then knit them in this order.

C7B: Slip next 7 sts from LH to RH needle p-wise, dropping extra loops made on the previous row, slip them back to LH needle and pass last 4 of these sts over the first 3 and then knit them in this order.

Standard abbreviations appear on page 71.

15, 16, 16) cm, ending with WS facing for next row.
Work 1 row in rib, dec 2 sts at the end of the row. 41 (41, 45, 49, 49, 53, 57, 57) sts.

Change to 3.5mm needles and begin lace patt as foll:
Row 1 (RS): K1, *yo, K3, yo, K1; rep from * to end.
Rows 2 & 4: Purl.
Row 3: K2, Sl 1, K2tog, psso, *K3, Sl 1, K2tog, psso; rep from * to last 2 sts, K2.
Work straight in lace patt until Front measures approx 32 (33, 34, 35, 36, 37, 37.5, 37.5) cm from cast-on edge, ending with a 4th row.

SHAPE ARMHOLES
Keeping patt correct, cast off as foll for your size:
Sizes 8 (10, 12): Cast off 4 sts at the beg of the next RS row, 3 sts on the foll 1 (1, 2) RS rows, 2 sts on the next 1 (2, 1) RS rows and 1 st at the beg of the next 2 (1, 1) RS rows. 30 (29, 32) sts.
Sizes 14 (16, 18): Cast off 4 sts at the beg of the next 1 (1, 2) RS rows, 3 sts on the foll RS row, 2 sts on the next 2 (3, 2) rows and 1 st at the beg of the next 3 (2, 2) rows. 35 (34, 36) sts.
Sizes 20 (22): Cast off 5 sts at the beg of the next RS row, 4 sts on the foll 1 (2) RS rows, 3 sts at the beg of the next 2 (1) RS rows, 2 sts on the foll 1 (2) RS rows and 1 st at the beg of the next 2 (1) rows. 38 (36) sts.

Work 2 more rows, you should have the WS facing for next row and be ready to work a 4th row of the patt.

Work increases ready for Mock Cable patt as foll:
Next row: P4 (1, 4, 4, 1, 2, 5, 2), *M1, P2; rep from * to last 2 (0, 2, 3, 1, 0, 3, 0) sts, M0 (0, 0, 0, 1, 0, 0, 0), P2 (0, 2, 3, 1, 0, 3, 0). 42 (43, 45, 49, 51, 53, 53, 53) sts.

SET MOCK CABLE PATTERN
Size 8 (14)
Row 1: P4 (3) *K7, P2; rep from * to last 2 (1) sts, P2 (1).
Row 2: K4 (3) *P7 wrapping yarn twice for each st, K2; rep from * to last 2 (1) sts, K2 (1).
Size 10 (16)
Row 1: P1 *P1, K7; rep from * to last 2 sts, P2.

Row 2: K2 *P7, wrapping yarn twice for each st, K1; rep from * to last st, K1.
Sizes 12 (18, 20, 22)
Row 1: K2 *P1, K7; rep from * to last 3 sts, P1, K2.
Row 2: P2, K1, *P7, wrapping yarn twice for each st, K1; rep from * to last 2 sts, P2.

Work in patt as set with row repeats as for Back, working Mock Cables as **C7F** until Front meas 10 (10, 10, 11, 11, 12, 12, 13) cm, from beg of armhole shaping, ending with WS facing for neck shaping.

Keeping patt correct throughout, cast off 5 sts at start of next row and then cast off 4 sts at start of next WS row, followed by casting off 3 sts at start of next 1 (1, 1, 2, 2, 2, 2, 2) WS rows. Cast off 2 sts at start of next 2 (2, 2, 1, 1, 2, 2, 2) WS rows. Finally, cast off 1 st at start of next 2 (2, 2, 3, 3, 3, 3, 3) WS rows. 24 (25, 27, 29, 31, 31, 31, 31) sts.

Now work straight until Front matches Back to shoulder shaping, cast off 8 (8, 9, 9, 10, 10, 10, 10) sts at the beginning of the next RS row, 8 (8, 9, 10, 10, 10, 10, 10) sts on foll RS row, cast off rem 8 (9, 9, 10, 11, 11, 11, 11) sts.

Right Front
Cast on 43 (43, 47, 51, 51, 55, 59, 59) sts using 3mm needles.
Row 1 (RS): K3, *P2, K2; rep from * to end.
Row 2: *P2, K2; rep from * to last 3 sts, P3.
These 2 rows set rib. Cont to work in rib until piece meas 14 (14, 14, 15, 15, 15, 16, 16) cm, ending with WS facing for next row.
Work 1 row in rib, dec 2 sts at the end of the row. 41 (41, 45, 49, 49, 53, 57, 57) sts.

Change to 3.5mm needles and begin lace patt:
Row 1 (RS): *K1, yo, K3, yo; rep from * to last st, K1.
Rows 2 & 4: Purl.
Row 3: K2, *Sl 1, K2tog, psso, K3; rep from * to last 5 sts, Sl 1, K2tog, psso, K2.
Work straight until Front meas approx 32 (33, 34, 35, 36, 37, 37.5, 37.5) cm from cast-on edge, ending with a 1st row.
Work remainder of Right Front as for Left Front but rev shapings as foll:
Work armhole cast offs on WS rows.

Work only 1 row before increasing for the Mock Cable patt, thus working increases on what would be a 4th lace row.

Set Mock Cable patt as for Left Front, but then work mock cables as **C7B**. Cast off neck sts at start of RS rows. Cast off shoulder stitches at start of WS rows.

Sleeves
Make 2 alike
Cast on 50 (50, 54, 54, 58, 58, 62, 62) sts using 3mm needles.
Row 1 (RS): K2, *P2, K2; rep from * to end.
Row 2: *P2, K2; rep from * to last 2 sts, P2.
These 2 rows set rib. Cont to work in rib until piece meas 15 (15, 15, 15, 16, 16, 16, 16) cm, ending with WS facing for next row.
Work 1 row in rib, dec 1 st on this row. 49 (49, 53, 53, 57, 57, 61, 61) sts.

Change to 3.5mm needles and begin lace patt:
Row 1 (RS): K1, *yo, K3, yo, K1; rep from * to end.
Rows 2 & 4: Purl.
Row 3: K2, Sl 1, K2tog, psso, *K3, Sl 1, K2tog, psso; rep from * to last 2 sts, K2.
Work in patt as set, inc 1 st each end of 29th (21st, 29th, 21st, 21st, 19th, 19th, 15th) and every foll 30th (24th, 30th, 24th, 24th, 20th, 20th, 16th) rows to 55 (57, 59, 61, 65, 67, 71, 73) sts.
Work inc rows: K1, M1, patt to last st, M1, K1.

Now work straight until Sleeve meas 46 (46, 47, 47, 48, 47, 46.5, 47) cm from cast-on edge.

SHAPE SLEEVEHEAD
Keeping patt correct, work dec as foll:
Row 1: K2, K2tog, patt to last 4 sts, SSK, K2. 53 (55, 57, 59, 63, 65, 69, 71) sts.
Rows 2, 3, 4 & 6: Work straight, in patt.
Row 5: As Row 1.
Rep these 6 rows 5 (6, 6, 7, 5, 7, 8, 9) times more. 31 (29, 31, 29, 41, 35, 35, 33) sts.
Now dec 1 st at each end of every RS row until 23 (23, 23, 25, 25, 25, 27, 29) sts rem.

Cast off rem sts.

Front bands and neckband

Block all pieces gently to measurements. Soak pieces in tepid water for 20 minutes. Squeeze gently and place between towels. Press to remove excess water. Lay a large towel on a flat surface, into which you can pin (carpet or foam tiles work well). Spread out the pieces to measurements and pin out to dry. When completely dry, sew shoulder seams.

With RS facing and 3mm circular needle, pick up and knit 32 (32, 32, 34, 34, 34, 36, 36) sts up front rib, 61 (64, 66, 65, 70, 74, 74, 75) up lace front, **marking the last** of these sts picked up, pick up and knit 33 (33, 33, 35, 35, 37, 37, 37) up right front neck, knit across 46 (47, 47, 52, 51, 55, 55, 55) sts held for back neck, pick up and knit 33 (33, 33, 35, 35, 37, 37, 37) sts down left front neck, 61 (64, 66, 65, 70, 74, 74, 75) down left front lace panel **marking the 1st** of this set of sts and finally 32 (32, 32, 34, 34, 34, 36, 36) sts down left front rib. 298 (305, 309, 320, 329, 345, 349, 351) sts.

Row 1 (WS): Knit.
Row 2: Knit to 1st marked st, *M1, knit marked st, M1* knit to 2nd marked st; rep from * to * then knit to end.
Row 3: As Row 1.
Row 4: As Row 2. 306 (313, 317, 328, 337, 353, 357, 359) sts.

Sizes 8 & 20 only
Work rows 1 & 2 once more. 310 (361) sts.

All Sizes
WS of work is now facing, cast off knitwise fairly loosely and evenly.

Making up

Mark button positions and sew on buttons, the 1st at top of rib, the rem 4 spaced approx 2.5cm apart below this.
Make button loops – with 3mm crochet hook make 8chst, join to a ring, cut yarn and use to sew onto band to match button placement. Sewn button loops can also be used, if preferred.

Match cast-off sts at top of sleevehead to shoulder seam and sew sleevehead into armhole. Join side and sleeve seams in one. Weave in all ends.

Hendred hat

by Elly Doyle

A cheeky hat, ideal for a long walk.

Skills
Working in the round

Size
To fit an adult woman
Head circumference approx 50-55cm
(19½-21½in)

Yarn
Fyberspates Scrumptious DK/Worsted
(45% silk, 55% merino; 100g skeins)
Purple (101) 1 x 100g skein

Needles and accessories
1 set 4mm (UK 8/US 6) double-pointed
needles (DPNs)
1 set 3.75mm (UK 9/US 5) DPNs
Set of spare DPNs approx 3.75mm (UK
9/US 5) or smaller
Stitch markers
Waste DK yarn

Tension
22 sts and 44 rounds to 10cm over
garter stitch in the round using 4mm
needles

Special abbreviations
Sl 1: Slip 1 stitch as if to purl, with yarn
at back of work

Standard abbreviations appear on
page 71.

Hat
BRIM
Using 3.75mm DPNs and waste
DK yarn, cast on 100 sts. Join to
work in the round, taking care not to
twist stitches and place marker for
start of round.
Change to main yarn.
Round 1: *K2, P2; rep from * to end
of round.
Last round sets 2 x 2 rib. Work 7 more
rounds in 2 x 2 rib.

Change to 4mm needles.
Round 9: Knit.

Change to 3.75mm needles.
Work 8 more rounds in 2 x 2 rib as set
previously.

Carefully remove the waste yarn from
the cast-on edge and pick up the
resulting main yarn stitches with a
set of spare needles. 100 sts on spare
needles as well as 100 sts on main
needles.
Fold the brim along the knit round, so
that the cast-on stitches are behind
the working stitches.
*Knit together one stitch from front
needle with one stitch from rear
needle; rep from * to end of round,
thus creating a folded brim. 100 sts.

Main section
Change to 4mm needles.
Next round: *K1, KFB; rep from * to
end of round. 150 sts.
Round 1: *Sl 1, P14; rep from * to end
of round.
Round 2: Knit.
These 2 rounds set garter stitch in
the round with slip stitch ribs. Cont to
work in patt as set until piece meas
9cm (not including brim), ending with
a knit round.

SHAPE CROWN
Rounds 1 to 3: Work in pattern as set.
Round 4: *K13, K2tog, pm; rep from *
to end of round. 140 sts.
Round 5: *Sl 1, purl to marker, slm; rep
from * to end of round.
Round 6: Knit.
Round 7: As round 5.
Round 8: *Knit to 2 sts before next
marker, K2tog; rep from * to end of
round. 130 sts.
Repeat Rounds 5-8 9 more times.
40 sts.
Then work Rounds 7 & 8 twice more
(so that decreases are worked on
alternate rounds instead of on 4th
rounds). 20 sts.
Next round: K1, [K2tog] 9 times, knit
together last st of round with first st of
next round. 10 sts.
Next round: [K2tog] 5 times. 5 sts.
Cut yarn and draw end through all
stitches to fasten off.

Weave in all ends.

Hendred mittens

by Elly Doyle

Mittens to match the hat, for complete cosiness.

Skills
Working in the round on DPNs

Size
To fit hand circumference 17-20cm (6½-8in)

Yarn
Fyberspates Scrumptious DK/Worsted (45% silk, 55% merino; 100g skeins) Purple (101) 1 x 100g skein

Needles and accessories
1 set 3mm (UK 11/US 2-3) double-pointed needles (DPNs)
Stitch markers

Tension
27 sts and 54 rounds to 10cm over garter stitch in the round using 3mm needles

Special abbreviations
Sl 1: Slip 1 stitch as if to purl, with yarn at back of work

Standard abbreviations appear on page 71.

Mitten

CUFF
Cast on 44 sts and distribute sts evenly over 3 or 4 DPNs. Join to work in the round, taking care not to twist the sts and place marker for start of round.
Rounds 1-6: Purl.
Round 7: *K2, P2; rep from * to end of round.
Last round sets 2 x 2 rib. Work 24 more rounds in rib as set.

THUMB GUSSET
Round 1: PFB, purl to end of round. 45 sts.
Round 2: Knit.
Round 3: Purl.
Round 4: K1, pm, M1, K1, M1, pm, knit to end of round. 47 sts.
Round 5: Purl.
Round 6: Knit.
Round 7: P1, slm, M1, purl to next marker, M1, slm, purl to end of round. 49 sts.
Round 8: Knit.
Round 9: Purl.
Round 10: K1, slm, M1, knit to next marker, M1, slm, knit to end of round. 51 sts.
Repeat last 6 rounds once more. 55 sts.
Then work rounds 5-8 once more. 57 sts.

Next round: P16 and place last 15 sts worked onto waste yarn or stitch holders for thumb. Purl to end of round, remove marker, P1. 42 sts.
Cast on 3 sts and place marker for new start of round. 45 sts.

PALM
Cont working in garter stitch in the round (alt knit and purl rounds), until 5cm short of desired length, ending with a knit round.
Piece should meas approx 20cm from cast-on edge.
Round 1: *Sl 1, P4; rep from * to end of round.
Round 2: Knit.
These 2 rounds set garter and slip stitch pattern. Work these 2 rounds 3 more times.

TOP DECREASES
Round 1: *Sl 1, P4; rep from * to end of round.
Round 2: *K3, K2tog; rep from * to end of round. 36 sts.
Round 3: *Sl 1, P3; rep from * to end of round.
Round 4: *K2, K2tog; rep from * to end of round. 27 sts.
Round 5: *Sl 1, P2; rep from * to end of round.
Round 6: Knit.
Rounds 7 & 8: As rounds 5 & 6.
Round 9: As round 5.
Round 10: *K1, K2tog; rep from * to end of round. 18 sts.
Round 11: *Sl 1, P1; rep from * to end of round.
Round 12: K1, [K2tog] 8 times, knit together last st of round with first st of next round. 9 sts.
Rounds 13 & 14: Knit.
Round 15: [K2tog] 4 times, K1. 5 sts.
Cut yarn and draw end through all stitches to fasten off.

THUMB
Return 15 sts on waste yarn to 3mm needles. Pick up and purl 3 sts along cast-on edge and place marker for start of round. 18 sts.

Next round: Knit.
Next round: Purl.
These 2 rounds set garter stitch in the round. Work in garter stitch until thumb meas 4cm or until 1cm less than desired thumb length, ending with a purl round.

Next round: *K4, K2tog; rep from * to end of round. 15 sts.
Next round: *P3, P2tog; rep from * to end of round. 12 sts.
Next round: *K2, K2tog; rep from * to end of round. 9 sts.
Next round: [P2tog] 4 times, P1. 5 sts.
Cut yarn and draw end through all stitches to fasten off.
Weave in all ends.

Make second mitten in the same way.

Wytham

by Jeni Hewlett

A lovely cardigan with V-neckline and lace trim.

Skills
Simple lace

Size

To fit bust

8-10	12-14	16-18	20-22	22-24	
81-86	91-96	101-107	112-117	122-127	cm
32-34	36-38	40-42	44-46	48-50	in

Actual bust

85	93	109	117	125	cm
33½	36½	43	46	49	in

Actual length

61	62	63	65.5	66	cm
24	24½	25	25½	26	in

Sleeve seam

40.5	42	42	43	43	cm
16	16½	16½	17	17	in

Yarn
Fyberspates Scrumptious DK/Worsted
(45% silk, 55% merino; 100g skeins)
Teal (106) 4 (5, 5, 6, 6) x 100g skeins

Needles and accessories
1 set 4.5mm (UK 7/US 7) circular
needles, 60cm long (long straight
needles are also suitable)
Stitch holders
Optional: 5 clear snap fasteners,
approx 7mm

Tension
20 sts and 28 rows to 10cm over st st
using 4.5mm needles
1 rep of Ostrich Lace meas 7cm wide
by 11.5cm tall using 4.5mm needles

Abbreviations
Standard abbreviations appear on
page 71.

Stitch Patterns

OSTRICH LACE
Worked over a multiple of 16 sts
+1, and over 32 rows. Also shown
on Chart.
Row 1 (RS): K1, *[yo, K1] twice, yo,
SSK twice, Sl 2, K1, p2sso, K2tog
twice, [yo, K1] 3 times; rep from *
to end.
Row 2 (WS): Purl.
Row 3: Knit.
Row 4: Purl.
Rows 5-16: Rep Rows 1-4, 3 times.
Row 17: K2tog, *K2tog twice, [yo, K1]
5 times, yo, SSK twice, Sl 2, K1, p2sso;
rep from * to last 15 sts, K2tog twice,
[yo, K1] 5 times, yo, SSK 3 times.
Row 18: Purl.
Row 19: Knit.
Row 20: Purl.
Rows 21-32: Rep Rows 17-20 3 times.

MOSS STITCH
Row 1 (RS): *K1, P1; rep from * to last
st, K1.
Row 2 (WS): *K1, P1; rep from * to last
st, K1.

Body
Using 4.5mm needles, cast on 171 (187,
219, 235, 251) sts.
Row 1 (RS): Work 5 sts in moss st, work
Row 1 of Ostrich Lace to last 5 sts,
work in moss stitch to end.
Row 2 (WS): Work 5 sts in moss st,
work Row 2 of Ostrich Lace to last 5
sts, work in moss stitch to end.
Last 2 rows set Ostrich Lace with moss
stitch borders. Work in patt as set until
2 reps of Ostrich Lace pattern have
been completed (64 rows in total).

Starting with a knit row, now cont in
st st, maintaining moss stitch at each
edge, until piece measures 39.5 (39.5,
39.5, 40.5, 40.5) cm from cast-on
edge, ending with RS facing for next
row. Break yarn.

Place first and last 43 (47, 55, 59, 63)
sts onto holders for Fronts.

Back
Join yarn to remaining 85 (93, 109, 117,
125) sts with RS facing.

SHAPE ARMHOLES
Working only in st st, cast off 5 (6, 7, 8,
8) sts at beg of next 2 rows. 75 (81, 95,
101, 109).
For 3rd, (4th, 5th) sizes only
Cast off 3 (3, 4) sts at beg of next 2
rows. 89 (95, 101) sts.
All sizes
Dec 1 st at each end of next and
foll 4 (5, 6, 7, 8) alt rows. 65 (69, 75,
79, 83,) sts.

Now work straight in st st until
armhole measures 19.5 (20.5, 21.5,
23, 23.5) cm, ending with RS facing
for next row.

SHAPE SHOULDERS
Cast off 6 (6, 7, 7, 7) sts at beg of next 2
rows. 53 (57, 61, 65, 69) sts.
Work to end of Back in moss stitch
only.
Cast off 6 (6, 7, 7, 8) sts at beg of next 2
rows. 41 (45, 47, 51, 53) sts.
Cast off 6 (7, 7, 8, 8) sts at beg of next 2
rows. 29 (31, 33, 35, 37) sts.
Cast off rem sts.

Right Front
Return 43 (47, 55, 59, 63) sts for Right
Front to needles. Join yarn with RS
facing and work as foll:
Next row (RS): Moss stitch over 5 sts,
knit to end.

SHAPE ARMHOLE
Keeping patt corr, cast off 5 (6, 7, 8, 8)
sts at beg of next row. 38 (41, 48, 51,
55) sts.
For 3rd (4th, 5th) sizes only
Patt 1 row, cast off 3 (3, 4) sts at beg of
next row. 45 (48, 51) sts.
All sizes
Dec 1 st at end of next and foll 4 (5, 6,
7, 8) alt rows, and **at the same time**,
when armhole measures 2.5cm, shape
neck as foll:
Dec 1 st at neck edge of next 7 (8, 9,
10, 11) RS rows, then on every 4th row

8 times. 18 (19, 21, 22, 23) sts.
Work neck decs thus: Work 5 sts in moss stitch, SSK, knit to end (shaping armhole if required).

Continue in st st with moss stitch border until armhole measures 19.5 (20.5, 21.5, 23, 23.5)cm, ending with WS facing for next row.

SHAPE SHOULDER
Cast off 6 (6, 7, 7, 7) sts at beg of next row. 12 (13, 14, 15, 16) sts.
Work 1 row.
Cast off 6 (6, 7, 7, 8) sts at beg of next row. 6 (7, 7, 8, 8) sts.
Work 1 row.
Cast off rem sts.

Left Front
Return 43 (47, 55, 59, 63) sts for Left Front to needles. Join yarn with RS facing.

SHAPE ARMHOLE
Next row (RS): Cast off 5 (6, 7, 8, 8) sts, knit to last 5 sts, work 5 sts in moss stitch. 38 (41, 48, 51, 55) sts.
Patt 1 row.
For 3rd (4th, 5th) sizes only
Cast off 3 (3, 4) sts at beg of next row. 45 (48, 51) sts.
Patt 1 row.
All sizes
Dec 1 st at beg of next and foll 4 (5, 6, 7, 8) alt rows, and **at the same time**, when armhole measures 2.5cm shape neck as foll:
Dec 1 st at neck edge of next 7 (8, 9, 10, 11) RS rows, then on every 4th row 8 times. 18 (19, 21, 22, 23) sts.
Work neck decs thus: Knit to last 7 sts (shaping armhole if required), K2tog, work 5 sts in moss stitch.

Continue in st st with moss stitch border until armhole measures 19.5 (20.5, 21.5, 23, 23.5) cm, ending with RS facing for next row.

SHAPE SHOULDER
Cast off 6 (6, 7, 7, 7) sts at beg of next row. 12 (13, 14, 15, 16) sts.
Work 1 row.
Cast off 6 (6, 7, 7, 8) sts at beg of next row. 6 (7, 7, 8, 8) sts.
Work 1 row.
Cast off rem sts.

Key

- ☐ Knit on RS, Purl on WS
- ⟍ SSK on RS
- ⟋ K2tog on RS
- ⋀ Sl 2 as if to K2tog, K1, p2sso
- ⦿ Yarnover
- ☐ Pattern repeat

Chart: Ostrich Lace

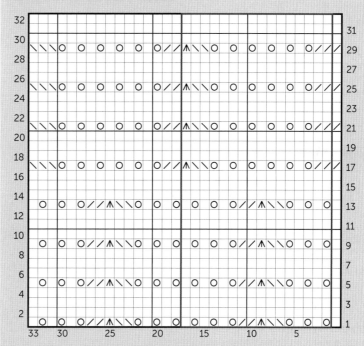

Measurements

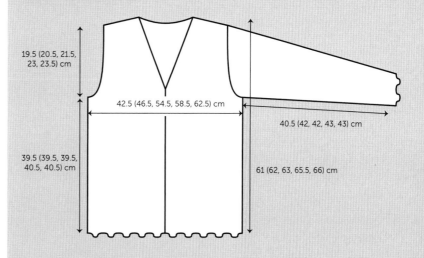

19.5 (20.5, 21.5, 23, 23.5) cm

42.5 (46.5, 54.5, 58.5, 62.5) cm

40.5 (42, 42, 43, 43) cm

39.5 (39.5, 39.5, 40.5, 40.5) cm

61 (62, 63, 65.5, 66) cm

Sleeves

Make 2 alike

Cast on 65 (65, 65, 65, 81) sts.

Work Rows 1-32 of Ostrich Lace once.

Next row (RS): K0 (1, 4, 1, 2), * K3 (3, 3, 4, 4), K2tog; rep from * to last 0 (4, 6, 4, 7) sts, K0 (4, 6, 4, 7). 52 (53, 54, 55, 69) sts.

Cont in st st and inc 1 st at each end of every 4th row 2 (4, 8, 12, 0) times, then on every 6th row 11 (10, 8, 6, 13) times. 78 (81, 86, 91, 95) sts.

Work straight in st st until sleeve meas 40.5 (42, 42, 43, 43) cm from cast-on edge, ending with RS facing for next row.

SHAPE SLEEVEHEAD

Cast off 5 (6, 7, 8, 8) sts at beg of next 2 rows. 68 (69, 72, 75, 79) sts.

For 3rd (4th, 5th) sizes only

Cast off 3 (3, 4) sts at beg of next 2 rows. 66 (69, 71) sts.

All sizes

Dec 1 st at each end of next row and foll 6 (7, 14, 15, 16) alt rows, then on every row 12 (12, 2, 2, 2) times. 30 (29, 32, 33, 33) sts.

Cast off 4 sts at beg of next 4 rows. 14 (13, 16, 17, 17) sts.

Cast off rem sts.

Finishing

Weave in ends but do not trim.

Soak cardigan in tepid water for 20 minutes. Squeeze gently and place between towels. Press to remove excess water. Lay a large towel on a flat surface, into which you can pin (carpet or foam tiles work well). Spread out the cardigan to measurements and pin out to dry. When completely dry, unpin and trim ends.

Join shoulder seams. Set sleevehead into armhole, matching centre of cast-off sts at top of sleevehead to shoulder seam and cast-off sts at armhole to cast-off sts at start of sleevehead shaping. Join sleeve seams.

Weave in all ends.

Sew snap fasteners to front bands if desired.

Murcott

by Jen Arnall-Culliford

A flattering wrap-around cardigan with short sleeves and clever pleated detailing.

Skills

Short rows, pleats and knitted-on edging

Size

To fit bust

8	10	12	14	16	18	20	22	
81	86	91	97	102	107	112	117	cm
32	34	36	38	40	42	44	46	in

Actual bust

88	93	98	103	108	113	118	123	cm
34½	36½	38½	40½	42½	44½	46½	48½	in

Actual length

53	55	56	57	58	60	61	62	cm
21	21½	22	22½	23	23½	24	24½	in

Sleeve Seam

All sizes: **7.5cm**, 3in

Yarn

Fyberspates Scrumptious DK/Worsted (45% silk, 55% merino; 100g skeins) Water (107) 4 (4, 5, 5, 5, 6, 6, 6) x 100g skeins

Needles and accessories

1 pair 4.5mm (UK 7/US 7) knitting needles
1 pair 4mm (UK 8/US 6) knitting needles
1 set 4.5mm (UK 7/US 7) circular needles, 80cm long
1 set 4mm (UK 7/US 7) double-pointed needles (DPNs)
Small quantity of waste DK yarn

Tension

21 sts and 26 rows to 10cm over st st using 4.5mm needles after washing and blocking

Special abbreviations

w&t: Wrap and turn. Take yarn to opp side of work (between the needles), slip next stitch purlwise from LH to RH needle, return yarn to original side of work, return slipped stitch to LH needle without twisting. The stitch is now wrapped with yarn. Turn work and start next row leaving any remaining stitches unworked. When this stitch is eventually worked, knit (or purl) the wrap and the stitch together as one stitch.

P2togE: Purl together 1 edging stitch with 1 stitch picked up from fronts. This joins the edging to the fronts with no need for seaming.

2 Stitch right pleat: Slip next 2 sts to first spare DPN, slip next 2 sts to second spare DPN. Fold DPNs in front of main LH needle so that the first DPN and the main needle are RS together, and the sts on the first and second DPNs are WS facing towards each other. Put RH needle through first stitch on front (first spare) DPN, middle (second spare) DPN and rear (main) needle and knit all 3 sts together. Repeat for second stitch on all 3 needles. This completes a 2 stitch right pleat. Decreases 6 sts to 2 sts.

3 Stitch right pleat: As above, but slip 3 sts to each DPN, and then repeat for second and third stitches on all 3 needles. Decreases 9 sts to 3 sts.

2 Stitch left pleat: Slip next 2 sts to first spare DPN and following 2 sts to second spare DPN. Fold the DPNs behind the LH needle (this time the sts on DPNs are RS facing each other). Put RH needle through first stitch on front (main) needle, middle (second) DPN and rear (first) DPN and knit all 3 sts together. Repeat for second stitch on all 3 needles. Decreases 6 sts to 2 sts.

3 Stitch left pleat: As for 2 st left pleat, but slip 3 sts to each DPN, and then repeat for second and third sts on all 3 needles. Decreases 9 sts to 3 sts.

Standard abbreviations are on page 71.

Pattern notes

This garment requires you to knit together more than one set of live stitches to make folds in fabric (hems and pleats). The neckband is made by picking up stitches and the fabric is shaped by working short-rows.

Back

Using waste yarn and 4mm needles, cast on 92 (98, 102, 108, 112, 118, 124, 130) sts.
Work 2 rows in st st, starting with a knit row.
Change to main yarn and work 5 rows in st st, ending with WS facing for next row.
Change to 4.5mm needles and work a further 5 rows in st st, ending with RS facing for next row.

HEM

Take a spare 4mm needle and pick up the main yarn 'purl bump' loops where they meet the waste yarn. Carefully remove the waste yarn, ensuring that you have all 92 (98, 102, 108, 112, 118, 124, 130) sts on your 4mm needle. Fold the WS together, so that you have the 4.5mm needle in front of the 4mm needle and you have RS facing outwards.

Next row (RS): Using 4.5mm needles, knit together the first stitch on the front needle with the first stitch on the rear needle. Continue to do this along the row, until all stitches have been knitted together with their counterparts on the rear needle. 92 (98, 102, 108, 112, 118, 124, 130) sts.
Work straight in st st for 9 more rows (piece should meas 5cm from bottom edge of folded hem), ending with RS facing for next row.
Row 1 (RS dec): K2, SSK, knit to last 4 sts, K2tog, K2. 90 (96, 100, 106, 110, 116, 122, 128) sts.
Work 3 rows in st st without shaping.
Repeat last 4 rows 6 more times.
Work Row 1 once more. 76 (82, 86, 92, 96, 102, 108, 114) sts.

Murcott continued

Work straight in st st for 9 rows (piece should meas approx 19.5cm from bottom edge of folded hem), ending with RS facing for next row.

Row 1 (RS inc): K2, M1L, knit to last 2 sts, M1R, K2. 78 (84, 88, 94, 98, 104, 110, 116) sts.

Work 3 rows straight in st st without shaping.

Repeat last 4 rows 6 more times.

Work increase row once more. 92 (98, 102, 108, 112, 118, 124, 130) sts.

Piece should meas approx 30.5cm from bottom of folded hem.

Work straight in st st for 9 (11, 13, 13, 17, 19, 21, 23) more rows, ending with RS facing for next row (piece meas 34 (35, 36, 36, 37, 38, 39, 40) cm from bottom edge of folded hem).

SHAPE ARMHOLE

Cast off 4 (5, 5, 6, 6, 7, 7, 8) sts at start of next 2 rows. 84 (88, 92, 96, 100, 104, 110, 114) sts.

Dec 1 st at each end of next 1 (3, 3, 5, 3, 5, 5, 5) rows and on foll 1 (1, 1, 1, 1, 0, 2) 4th rows. 80 (80, 84, 84, 92, 92, 100, 100) sts.

Work straight until armhole meas 11 (12, 12, 13, 13, 14, 14, 14) cm, ending with RS facing for next row.

Pleat row (RS): K34 (34, 36, 36, 37, 37, 41, 41), work a 2 (2, 2, 2, 3, 3, 3, 3) st right pleat over next 6 (6, 6, 6, 9, 9, 9, 9) sts, then work a 2 (2, 2, 2, 3, 3, 3, 3) st left pleat over next 6 (6, 6, 6, 9, 9, 9, 9) sts, knit to end of row. 72 (72, 76, 76, 80, 80, 88, 88) sts.

Work straight in st st until armhole meas 18 (19, 19, 20, 20, 21, 21, 21) cm, ending with RS facing for next row.

SHAPE SHOULDER

Cast off 6 (6, 6, 6, 7, 7, 7, 7) sts at start of next 2 rows. 60 (60, 64, 64, 66, 66, 74, 74) sts.

Next row (RS): Cast off 6 (6, 6, 6, 6, 6, 7, 7) sts, knit until there are 9 (9, 10, 10, 10, 10, 12, 12) sts on RH needle. Place rem sts on a holder and continue on these 9 (9, 10, 10, 10, 10, 12, 12) sts only. Turn.

Next row (WS): Cast off 4 (4, 4, 4, 4, 4, 5, 5) sts and purl to end. 5 (5, 6, 6, 6, 6, 7, 7) sts.

Cast off rem sts.

Return to sts on holder and rejoin yarn with RS facing. Cast off centre 30 (30, 32, 32, 34, 34, 36, 36) sts and knit to end. 15 (15, 16, 16, 16, 16, 19, 19) sts.

Next row (WS): Cast off 6 (6, 6, 6, 6, 6, 7, 7) sts and purl to end. 9 (9, 10, 10, 10, 10, 12, 12) sts.

Next row (RS): Cast off 4 (4, 4, 4, 4, 4, 5, 5) sts and knit to end. 5 (5, 6, 6, 6, 6, 7, 7) sts.

Cast off rem sts.

Left Front

Using waste yarn and 4mm needles, cast on 84 (90, 94, 100, 104, 110, 116, 122) sts.

Work 2 rows in st st, starting with a knit row.

Change to main yarn and work 5 rows in st st, ending with WS facing for next row.

Change to 4.5mm needles and work a further 5 rows in st st, ending with RS facing for next row.

Take a spare 4mm needle and pick up the main yarn 'purl bump' loops where they meet the waste yarn. Carefully remove the waste yarn, ensuring that you have all 84 (90, 94, 100, 104, 110, 116, 122) sts on your 4mm needle. Fold the WS together, so that you have the 4.5mm needle in front of the 4mm needle and you have RS facing outwards.

Next row (RS): Using 4.5mm needle, knit together the first stitch on the front needle with the first stitch on the rear needle. Continue to do this along the row, until all stitches have been knitted together with their counterparts on the rear needle. 84 (90, 94, 100, 104, 110, 116, 122) sts.

Work straight in st st for 9 more rows (piece should meas 5cm from bottom edge of folded hem), ending with RS facing for next row.

** Row 1 (RS): K2, SSK, knit to end. 83 (89, 93, 99, 103, 109, 115, 121) sts.

Work 3 rows in st st without shaping.

Repeat last 4 rows 6 more times.

Work Row 1 once more. 76 (82, 86, 92, 96, 102, 108, 114) sts.

Work straight in st st for 9 rows (piece should meas approx 19.5cm from bottom edge of folded hem), ending with RS facing for next row.

SIDE AND NECK SHAPING

Read the following section carefully, as side and neck shaping are worked simultaneously.

Next row (RS): K2, M1L, knit to end. 77 (83, 87, 93, 97, 103, 109, 115) sts.

Inc 1 st at start of 7 foll 4th rows (all will be RS), then when piece meas same as Back to start of armhole shaping with RS facing for next row, work armholes as below, and **at the same time** work neck shaping as foll :

Cast off 9 (10, 11, 11, 11, 11, 12, 13) sts at start of next row (WS), cast off 6 (6, 6, 6, 6, 6, 7, 8) sts at start of foll WS row, cast off 5 sts, then 4 sts, then 3 sts at start of foll 3 WS rows. Then cast off 2 sts at start of next 6 (6, 7, 9, 9, 9, 10, 10) WS rows. Dec 1 st at start of foll 11 (13, 13, 12, 13, 16, 17, 18) WS rows and finally dec 1 st at start of 3 foll 4th rows (all will be WS).

SHAPE ARMHOLE

Continue to work neck shaping as previously described, and cast off 4 (5, 5, 6, 6, 7, 7, 8) sts at start of RS row, work 1 row straight at armhole edge, then dec 1 st at armhole edge on foll 1 (3, 3, 5, 3, 5, 5, 5) rows and on foll 1 (1, 1, 1, 1, 1, 0, 2) 4th rows.

Work straight at armhole edge until neck shaping is complete. 25 (25, 26, 26, 31, 31, 33, 33) sts.

Work straight until armhole meas 11 (12, 12, 13, 13, 14, 14, 14) cm, ending with RS facing for next row.

Pleat row (RS): K7, * work a 2 (2, 2, 2, 3, 3, 3, 3) st right pleat over next 6 (6, 6, 6, 9, 9, 9, 9) sts; rep from * once more, knit to end of row. 17 (17, 18, 18, 19, 19, 21, 21) sts.

Work straight until Front matches Back to start of shoulder shaping, ending with RS facing for next row.

Cast off 6 (6, 6, 6, 7, 7, 7, 7) sts at start of next row and cast off 6 (6, 6, 6, 6, 6, 7, 7) sts at start of foll alt row. 5 (5, 6, 6, 6, 6, 7, 7) sts.

Work 1 row straight.

Cast off rem sts.

Right Front

Work as for Left Front to **. 84 (90, 94, 100, 104, 110, 116, 122) sts.

** **Row 1 (RS):** Knit to last 4 sts, K2tog, K2. 83 (89, 93, 99, 103, 109, 115, 121) sts.
Work 3 rows in st st without shaping.
Rep last 4 rows 6 more times.
Work Row 1 once more. 76 (82, 86, 92, 96, 102, 108, 114) sts.
Work straight in st st for 9 rows (piece should meas approx 19.5cm from bottom edge of folded hem), ending with RS facing for next row.

SIDE AND NECK SHAPING

Read the following section carefully, as side and neck shaping are worked simultaneously.

Next row (RS): Cast off 9 (10, 11, 11, 11, 11, 12, 13) sts, knit to last 2 sts, M1R, K2. 68 (73, 76, 82, 86, 92, 97, 102) sts.
Inc 1 st at end of 7 foll 4th rows (all will be RS), then when piece meas same as Back to start of armhole shaping with WS facing for next row, work armholes as below, and **at the same time** work neck shaping as foll :
Cast off 6 (6, 6, 6, 6, 6, 7, 8) sts at start of foll RS row, cast off 5 sts, then 4 sts, then 3 sts at start of foll 3 RS rows.
Then cast off 2 sts at start of next 6 (6, 7, 9, 9, 9, 10, 10) RS rows. Dec 1 st at start of foll 11 (13, 13, 12, 13, 16, 17, 18) RS rows and finally dec 1 st at start of 3 foll 4th rows (all will be RS).

SHAPE ARMHOLE

Continue to work neck shaping as previously described, and cast off 4 (5, 5, 6, 6, 7, 7, 8) sts at start of WS row, then dec 1 st at armhole edge on foll 1 (3, 3, 5, 3, 5, 5, 5) rows and on foll 1 (1, 1, 1, 1, 1, 0, 2) 4th rows.
Work straight at armhole edge until neck shaping is complete. 25 (25, 26, 26, 31, 31, 33, 33) sts.

Work straight until armhole meas 11 (12, 12, 13, 13, 14, 14, 14) cm, ending with RS facing for next row.
Pleat row (RS): K6 (6, 7, 7, 6, 6, 8, 8), * work a 2 (2, 2, 2, 3, 3, 3, 3) st left pleat over next 6 (6, 6, 6, 9, 9, 9, 9) sts; rep from * once more, knit to end of row. 17 (17, 18, 18, 19, 19, 21, 21) sts.

Work straight until Front matches Back to start of shoulder shaping, ending with WS facing for next row.

Measurements

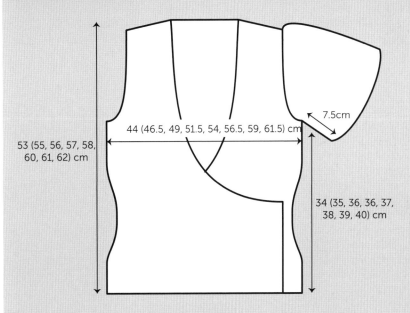

53 (55, 56, 57, 58, 60, 61, 62) cm

44 (46.5, 49, 51.5, 54, 56.5, 59, 61.5) cm

7.5cm

34 (35, 36, 36, 37, 38, 39, 40) cm

Cast off 6 (6, 6, 6, 7, 7, 7, 7) sts at start of next row and cast off 6 (6, 6, 6, 6, 6, 7, 7) sts at start of foll alt row. 5 (5, 6, 6, 6, 6, 7, 7) sts.
Work 1 row straight.
Cast off rem sts.

Sleeves
Make 2 alike
Using waste yarn and 4mm needles, cast on 100 (100, 104, 104, 108, 108, 112, 112) sts.
Work 2 rows in st st, starting with a knit row.
Change to main yarn and work 5 rows in st st, ending with WS facing for next row.
Change to 4.5mm needles and work a further 5 rows in st st, ending with RS facing for next row.

Take a spare 4mm needle and pick up the main yarn 'purl bump' loops where they meet the waste yarn. Carefully remove the waste yarn, ensuring that you have all 100 (100, 104, 104, 108, 108, 112, 112) sts on your 4mm needle. Fold the WS together, so that you have the 4.5mm needle in front of the 4mm needle and you have RS facing outwards.
Next row (RS): Using 4.5mm needle, knit together the first st on the front needle with the first st on the rear needle. Continue to do this along the row, until all stitches have been knitted together with their counterparts on the rear needle. 100 (100, 104, 104, 108, 108, 112, 112) sts.

Next row (WS): Purl to end.
Short row 1 (RS): Knit to last 40 sts, w&t, leaving all remaining sts unworked.
Short row 2 (WS): Purl to last 40 sts, w&t, leaving all remaining sts unworked.
Short row 3 (RS): Knit to last 30 sts (knitting wraps with sts when you reach them), w&t.
Short row 4 (WS): Purl to last 30 sts (purling wraps with sts when you reach them), w&t.
Short rows 5 & 6: Work in st st to last 20 sts (work wraps with sts as before), w&t.
Short rows 7 & 8: Work in st st to last 10 sts (work wraps with sts as before), w&t.

Next row (RS): Knit to end, working wraps with sts.
Next row (WS): Purl to end, working wraps with sts.

Next row (RS dec): K2, SSK, knit to last 4 sts, K2tog, K2. 98 (98, 102, 102, 106, 106, 110, 110) sts.
Dec 1 st at each end of foll RS rows 4 more times. 90 (90, 94, 94, 98, 98, 102, 102) sts.
Work 7 rows straight in st st, ending with RS facing for next row.

SHAPE SLEEVEHEAD
Cast off 4 (5, 5, 6, 6, 7, 7, 8) sts at start of next 2 rows. 82 (80, 84, 82, 86, 84, 88, 86) sts.
Cast off 3 (3, 4, 4, 4, 4, 4, 4) sts at start of next 2 rows. 76 (74, 76, 74, 78, 76, 80, 78) sts.
Dec 1 st at start of next 6 (14, 12, 18, 18, 24, 24, 26) rows. 70 (60, 64, 56, 60, 52, 56, 52) sts.
Dec 1 st at each end of next 14 (8, 10, 6, 6, 2, 2, 0) rows. 42 (44, 44, 44, 48, 48, 52, 52) sts.
Cast off 4 (4, 4, 4, 4, 4, 5, 5) sts at start of next 4 rows. 26 (28, 28, 28, 32, 32, 32, 32) sts.
Cast off rem sts.

Making up
Weave in ends but do not trim.
Soak sweater in tepid water for 20 minutes. Squeeze gently and place between towels. Press to remove excess water. Lay a large towel on a flat surface, into which you can pin (carpet or foam tiles work well). Spread out the sweater to measurements and pin out to dry. When completely dry, unpin and trim ends.
Sew shoulder seams.
Match centre of cast-off edge of sleevehead to shoulder seam and match cast-off sts at start of armhole to cast-off sts at start of sleevehead shaping. Sew sleevehead into armhole easing the fullness to top of shoulder. You may find it helpful to add a gathering thread before sewing the sleevehead into place.

Fold a strip 4 sts wide at open edge of each front to WS and slipstitch in place.

Edging and ties
Cast on 8 sts using 4.5mm needles.
Row 1 (RS): *K1, P1; rep from * to end.
Row 2 (WS): As Row 1.
These 2 rows set 1 x 1 rib. Cont in rib until tie meas 58 (60, 63, 65, 68, 70, 73, 75) cm, ending with WS facing for next row, do not cast off.

Using a long 4.5mm circular needle, and starting at top of folded seam on left front, pick up but do not knit 62 (64, 67, 69, 70, 73, 77, 79) sts along left front neck edge up to shoulder seam, 26 (26, 26, 26, 28, 28, 32, 32) sts along back neck, and 62 (64, 67, 69, 70, 73, 77, 79) sts from right shoulder seam down right neck edge. 150 (154, 160, 164, 168, 174, 186, 190) sts picked up.

Slip 8 sts of tie onto end of circular needle at left front edge, so that WS of cardigan and WS of tie are both facing. Work as foll:
Next row (WS): [K1, P1] 3 times, K1, P2togE (this joins 1 rib st with the 1st st picked up at left front).
Next row (RS): Sl 1, P1, [K1, P1] 6 times. Turn.
Next row: [K1, P1] 3 times, K1, P2togE. Turn.
Repeat last 2 rows until edging has been worked around the whole neck edge and no picked up stitches remain.
Cont to work in 1 x 1 rib on rem 8 sts until tie meas 88 (90, 93, 95, 98, 100, 103, 105) cm from end of right front. Cast off.

Sew side and sleeve seams in one, leaving a gap of 4cm at right side seam, level with tie.

Filkins

by Jen Arnall-Culliford

Linked circles form a memorable, quirky wrap.

Pattern notes

This scarf is created by knitting a string of circles. The second (and third) strings are then joined to each other by knitting a picked-up stitch together with a working stitch 5 times on the ends of central circle rows.

Scarf

FIRST CIRCLE STRING

Cast on 5 sts.

Row 1 (RS): KFB, knit to last stitch, KFB. 7 sts.

Rows 2-5: As row 1. 15 sts.

Row 6: Knit.

Row 7: KFB, knit to last stitch, KFB. 17 sts.

Rows 8-10: Knit.

Row 11: KFB, knit to last stitch, KFB. 19 sts.

Rows 12-24: Knit.

Row 25: K1, SSK, knit to last 3 sts, K2tog, K1. 17 sts.

Rows 26-28: Knit.

Row 29: As row 25. 15 sts.

Row 30: Knit.

Rows 31-35: As row 25. 5 sts.

Row 36: Knit.

Rows 1 to 36 set circle pattern. Work a further 10 (14) repeats of circle pattern, to create a string of 11 (15) circles. Work rows 1-34 of circle pattern once more.

Final row: K1, SSK, pass second stitch on RH needle over first to cast it off, K1, pass second st over first to cast off, K2tog, pass second st over first to cast off, K1, pass second st over first to cast off. Break yarn and pass through remaining stitch to fasten off. This makes your first string of 12 (16) circles in total.

SECOND CIRCLE STRING

Cast on 5 sts.

Row 1 (RS): KFB, knit to last stitch, KFB. 7 sts.

Rows 2-5: As row 1. 15 sts.

Row 6: Knit.

Row 7: KFB, knit to last stitch, KFB. 17 sts.

Rows 8-10: Knit.

Row 11: KFB, knit to last stitch, KFB. 19 sts.

Rows 12: Knit.

Row 13: With yarn in back, pick up 1 st from end of same row of circle on first string (hold first string with RS facing), K2tog to join first string to second string, knit to end.

Row 14: Knit.

Rows 15-22: Repeat rows 15 and 16 four more times.

Rows 23-24: Knit.

Row 25: K1, SSK, knit to last 3 sts, K2tog, K1. 17 sts.

Rows 26-28: Knit.

Row 29: As row 25. 15 sts.

Row 30: Knit.

Rows 31-35: As row 25. 5 sts.

Row 36: Knit.

Rows 1 to 36 set joining circles pattern. Work a further 10 (14) repeats of joining circles pattern to create a string of 11 (15) circles (joined to the first string).

Work rows 1-34 of joining circle pattern once more.

Final row: K1, SSK, pass second stitch on RH needle over first to cast it off, K1, pass second st over first to cast off, K2tog, pass second st over first to cast off, K1, pass second st over first to cast off. Break yarn and pass through remaining stitch to fasten off.

THIRD CIRCLE STRING
(Large wrap only)

Work as second circle string.

Finishing

Weave in all ends and block gently to measurements.

Skills

Garter stitch with shaping

Size

Medium (2 x 12 circles): Approx 22cm x 140cm (8½in x 55in)
Large (3 x 16 circles): Approx 32cm x 180cm (12½in x 71in)

Yarn

Fyberspates Scrumptious Aran (45% silk, 55% merino; 100g skeins)
Rose Pink (408) 2 (4) x 100g skeins

Needles

1 pair 5mm (UK 6/US 8) needles

Tension

19 sts and 32 rows to 10cm over garter stitch using 5mm needles

Abbreviations

Standard abbreviations appear on page 71.

Diagram

⚪ Small size layout   ⚪ Large size layout

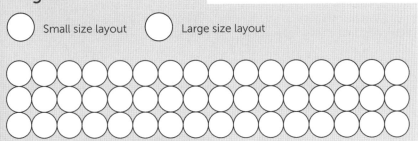

Hinksey

by Lily France

Beautiful mittens entwined with cables that meander across the back and thumb.

Skills

Cables and working in the round

Size

Lying flat, unstretched, 30cm (12in) from cuff to top and 8.5cm (3½in) wide [17cm (7in) circumference] at palm. When worn, 28cm (11in) from cuff to top and 20cm (8in) circumference at palm. Will comfortably stretch further, giving slightly less length.

Yarn

Fyberspates Scrumptious Aran (45% silk, 55% merino; 100g skeins)
Moss (402) 1 x 100g skein
If length is added, 2 skeins will be needed.

Needles and accessories

1 set 4mm (UK8/US 6) double-pointed needles (DPNs)
1 stitch marker
Cable needle (cn)

Tension

20 sts and 26 rows to 10cm over reverse st st

Special abbreviations

C4B: Slip 2 sts to cn and hold at back, K2; K2 from cn
T4B: Slip 2 sts to cn and hold at back, K2; P2 from cn
C4BP: Slip 2 sts to cn and hold at back, P2; P2 from cn
C4F: Slip 2 sts to cn and hold at front, K2; K2 from cn
T4F: Slip 2 sts tocn and hold at front, P2; K2 from cn
C4FP: Slip 2 sts to cn and hold at front, P2; P2 from cn
Standard abbreviations appear on page 71.

Pattern notes

This pattern uses charts to show the cable pattern. As the mittens are knitted in the round, each line of the charts is read from right to left.

Right Mitten

Cast on 44 sts using the long-tail cast-on method. Divide sts over DPNs and join to work in the round, taking care not to twist stitches. Place marker for start of round.
Round 1: [K2, P2] 11 times.
Repeat Round 1, 22 more times.
If you want more length, add extra rounds here, noting that you may need more yarn.
Begin working from **Chart A** (right mitten) Row 6, working across the back of hand sts then across the palm sts from right to left on all rounds. Continue to work from Chart A until Round 28 is complete. 62 sts.
Round 29: Work 24 sts in pattern, slip next 18 sts to waste yarn for thumb, work rem 20 sts of round from Chart A. 44 sts.
Rounds 30-35: Work from Chart A as set.
Repeat last 6 rounds 3 more times. Continue to work from Chart A from Round 36 to 41.
Round 42: You may need to rearrange the sts on your DPNs at this point, to enable decreases to be worked. Continue to work from Chart A until Round 49 is complete. 12 sts.

Turn mitten inside out and rearrange sts so that you have 6 palm sts on one needle and 6 back of hand sts on the other needle. Cast off using the 3-needle cast-off method.
Fasten off.

Left Mitten

Cast on 44 sts using the long-tail cast-on method. Divide sts over DPNs and join to work in the round, taking care not to twist stitches. Place marker for start of round.
Round 1: [K2, P2] 11 times.

Repeat Round 1, 22 more times.
If you want more length, add extra rounds here, noting that you may need more yarn.
Begin working from **Chart B** (left mitten) Row 6, working across the palm sts then across the back of hand sts from right to left on all rounds. Continue to work from Chart B until Round 28 is complete. 62 sts.
Round 29: Work 20 sts in pattern, slip next 18 sts to waste yarn for thumb, work rem 24 sts of round from Chart B. 44 sts.
Rounds 30-35: Work from Chart B as set.
Repeat last 6 rounds 3 more times. Continue to work from Chart B from Round 36 to 41.
Round 42: You may need to rearrange the sts on your DPNs at this point, to enable decreases to be worked. Continue to work from Chart B until Round 49 is complete. 12 sts.

Turn mitten inside out and rearrange sts so that you have 6 palm sts on one needle and 6 back of hand sts on the other needle. Cast off using the 3-needle cast-off method.
Fasten off and weave in ends.

Thumb

Work both thumbs alike
Return 18 sts on waste yarn to DPNs. With right side facing, rejoin yarn and work across sts as follows:
Round 1: [K2, P2] 4 times, K2, pick up and knit 4 sts across opening. 22 sts.
Round 2 (partial round): [K2, P2] twice, K1.
Place marker for beginning of round and redistribute sts between needles, if desired.
Work from Chart C Rows 1 to 16 inclusive. 6 sts.

Turn mitten inside out and rearrange sts so that you have 3 sts on each needle. Cast off using the 3-needle cast-off method.
Fasten off and weave in ends.

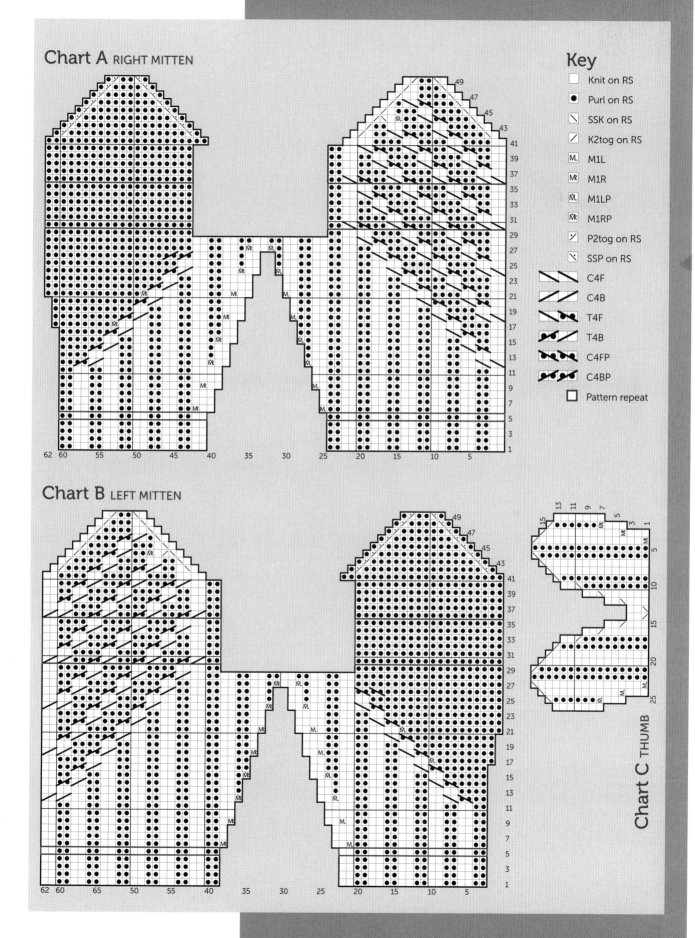

Chart A RIGHT MITTEN

Chart B LEFT MITTEN

Chart C THUMB

Key

☐	Knit on RS
●	Purl on RS
⟍	SSK on RS
⟋	K2tog on RS
M̲	M1L
M̲ʀ	M1R
M̲	M1LP
M̲ʀ	M1RP
⟋	P2tog on RS
⟍	SSP on RS
	C4F
	C4B
	T4F
	T4B
	C4FP
	C4BP
☐	Pattern repeat

Chinnor
by Jen Arnall-Culliford

Pretty stripes and a twisted rib pattern give a simple cowl star quality.

Pattern notes
Knitted flat, the row-end edges of this cosy cowl are seamed together once knitting is complete. Chinnor is simplicity itself, but gives very stylish results. Instant gratification knitting!

Cowl
Using Colour A and 5mm needles, cast on 104 sts.

Row 1: Sl 1, *P1, K1 tbl; rep from * to last st, P1.
Row 2: As row 1.
These two rows set twisted rib pattern.

Join in Colour B and work rows 1 and 2 again.

Cont to work in alternating 2 row stripes of Colours A and B, until piece meas 30cm from cast-on edge, ending with a Colour A stripe. Don't break off yarns after each stripe, just carry them up the side of the work.

Cast off all sts in pattern.
Sew row-end edges together to complete the cowl. Weave in all ends.

Skills
Simple knit and purl (and through the back of the loop) only

Size
To fit an adult.
Stretches to 58cm circumference, and 30cm tall

Yarn
Fyberspates Scrumptious Aran (45% silk, 55% merino; 100g skeins)
Colour A, Rose Pink (408) 1 x 100g skein
Colour B Moss (402) 1 x 100g skein

Needles
1 pair 5mm (UK 6/US 8) knitting needles

Tension
Unstretched: 26 sts and 24 rows to 10cm over twisted rib on 5mm needles
Gently stretched: 16 sts and 28 rows to 10cm over twisted rib on 5mm needles

Abbreviations
Standard abbreviations appear on page 71.

Longcot

by Jeni Hewlett

This casual jacket is like a big hug – warm and cosy.

Skills

Short-row shaping

Size

To fit bust

8-10	12-14	16-18	20-22	24-26	
81-86	92-97	102-107	112-117	122-127	cm
32-34	36-38	40-42	44-46	48-50	in

Actual bust (twice Back width)

84	94	106	114	126	cm
33	37	41½	45	49½	in

Length, without folding collar

78	78	80	82	82	cm
30½	30½	31½	32½	32½	in

Sleeve seam

43	43	45	46	46	cm
17	17	17¾	18	18	in

Yarn

Fyberspates Scrumptious Aran (45% silk, 55% merino; 100g skeins)
Water (403) 8 (9, 10, 11, 11) x 100g skeins

Needles and accessories

1 set 5mm (UK 6/US 8) circular knitting needles (due to large number of stitches), approx 80cm long
1 set 4mm (UK 8/US 6) circular knitting needles (due to large number of stitches), approx 80cm long

Tension (after blocking)

17 sts and 22 rows to 10cm in st st using 5mm needles
17 sts and 32 rows to 10cm in Moss Stitch using 4mm needles
17 sts and 25 rows to 10cm in 3x3 Rib using 5mm needles
17 sts and 26 rows to 10cm In Texture Stitch using 4mm needles
17 sts and 26 rows to 10cm in Garter Diagonals using 5mm needles

Special abbreviations

w&t: Wrap and turn. Take yarn to opp side of work (betw needles), slip next st pwise from LH to RH needle, return yarn to original side of work, return slipped st to LH needle without twisting. The st is now wrapped. Turn work and start next row leaving any remaining sts unworked. When this st is worked, knit (or purl) the wrap and the st together as one st.
Standard abbreviations appear on page 71.

Stitch patterns

MOSS STITCH - 4MM NEEDLES
Worked over 2 sts and 2 rows (4mm needles)
Row 1 (RS): *K1, P1; rep from * to end of row.
Row 2 (WS): *P1, K1; rep from * to end of row.

3X3 RIB - 5MM NEEDLES
Worked over multiple of 6 + 3 sts and 2 rows
Row 1 (RS): *K3, P3; rep from * to last 3 sts, K3.
Row 2 (WS): P3, *K3, P3; rep from * to end.

DOT STITCH - 5MM NEEDLES
Worked over 4 sts and 8 rows
Row 1 (RS): *K3, P1; rep from * to end.
Row 2 & all foll WS rows: Purl.
Row 3: Knit.
Row 5: K1, *P1, K3; rep from * to last 3 sts, P1, K2.
Row 7: Knit.
Row 8: As row 2.

TEXTURE STITCH - 4MM NEEDLES
Worked over 2 sts and 4 rows
Row 1 (RS): *K1, P1; rep from * to end.
Row 2 (WS): *K1, P1; rep from * to end.
Row 3: *P1, K1; rep from * to end.
Row 4: *P1, K1; rep from * to end.

GARTER DIAGONALS - 5MM NEEDLES
Worked over 4 sts and 8 rows
Row 1 and all foll RS rows: Knit.
Row 2 (WS): *K3, P1; rep from * to end.
Row 4: *K2, P1, K1; rep from * to end.
Row 6: *K1, P1, K2; rep from * to end.
Row 8: *P1, K3; rep from * to end.

Pattern notes

Worked from side to side, this waterfall-fronted cardigan uses short-row shaping to create the armholes. Fronts and back are knitted in one piece and sleeves are sewn in at the end.

Left Front

Using 4mm needles, cast on 132 (132, 136, 140, 140) sts using the cable cast-on method.
Work 50 rows in Moss Stitch.

Change to 5mm needles and work 32 rows in Garter Diagonals patt.

Change to 4mm needles and work 22 (28, 38, 42, 44) rows in Texture Stitch.

Change to 5mm needles and work 8 rows in Dot Stitch.

SHAPE ARMHOLE
**Row 1 (RS): Work 59 (63, 65, 70, 70) sts in patt, w&t.
Row 2 (WS): Patt to end of row.
Row 3: Work 55 (59, 61, 66, 66) sts in patt, w&t.
Row 4: Patt to end.
Row 5: Work 51 (55, 57, 62, 62) sts in patt, w&t.
Row 6: Patt to end.

Size 12-14 only
Next row: Work 51 sts in patt, w&t.
Next row: Patt to end.

Size 16-18 only
Next row: Work 55 sts in patt, w&t.
Next row: Patt to end.
Next row: Work 53 sts in patt, w&t.
Next row: Patt to end.

Sizes 20-22, 24-26 only
Next row: Work 60 sts in patt, w&t.
Next row: Patt to end.
Next row: Work 58 sts in patt, w&t.
Next row: Patt to end.
Next row: Work 56 sts in patt, w&t.
Next row: Patt to end.

All sizes
Next row: Work 51 (51, 53, 56, 56) sts

Longcot continued

in patt, then cast off next 39 (39, 41, 42, 42) sts, working wraps with sts when you reach them, place final 42 sts of row on a holder for collar.

With WS facing, rejoin yarn to first 51 (51, 53, 56, 56) sts and patt to end of row.
Work 4 (8, 12, 10, 14) more rows on these sts, slipping the first st on WS rows to make a firm edge for the armhole.

Size 12-14 only
Next row (RS): Patt to end, turn, cast on 4 sts. 55 sts.
Next row (WS): Patt to end.

Size 16-18 only
Next row (RS): Patt to end, turn, cast on 2 sts. 55 sts.
Next row (WS): Patt to end.
Rep last 2 rows once more. 57 sts.

Sizes 20-22, 24-26 only
Next row (RS): Patt to end, turn, cast on 2 sts. 58 sts.
Next row (WS): Patt to end.
Rep last 2 rows twice more. 62 sts.

All sizes
Row 1 (RS): Patt to end, turn, cast on 4 sts. 55 (59, 61, 66, 66) sts.
Row 2 (WS): Patt to end.
Row 3: Patt to end, turn, cast on 4 sts. 59 (63, 65, 70, 70) sts.
Row 4: Patt to end.

Row 5: Patt to end, turn, cast on 31 (27, 29, 28, 28) sts, join in 42 held collar sts, patt to end. 132 (132, 136, 140, 140) sts.
Row 6: Patt to end.**

Back
Work in Dot Stitch across all sts for a further 23 rows.
Next row (WS): Purl, increasing 3 (3, 5, 1, 1) sts evenly across row. 135 (135, 141, 141, 141) sts.
Work 25 (29, 35, 41, 49) rows in 3x3 rib.
Next row (WS): Work in rib as set, but decreasing 3 (3, 5, 1, 1) sts evenly across row. 132 (132, 136, 140, 140) sts.
Change to 4mm needles and work 26 rows in Moss Stitch.
Change to 5mm needles and work 8 rows in Dot Stitch.
Repeat armhole shaping from ** to **.

Right Front
Work in Dot Stitch pattern for 20 (26, 32, 36, 38) rows.
Work in Garter Diagonals pattern for 42 rows.
Change to 4mm needles and work in Moss Stitch for 50 rows.

Cast off all sts.

Sleeve
Make 2 alike
Using 5mm needles, cast on 58 (60, 64, 68, 72) sts using the cable cast-on method.

Knit 6 rows.
Starting with a knit row, work in st st for the remainder of the sleeve.
Increase 1 st at each end of 8th row 9 times. 76 (78, 82, 86, 90) sts.
Work straight for 20 (20, 24, 26, 26) rows.

SHAPE SLEEVEHEAD
Cast off 4 (5, 6, 7, 8) sts at start of next 2 rows. 68 (68, 70, 72, 74) sts.
Dec 1 st at each end of foll 10 (10, 10, 12, 14) rows. 48 (48, 50, 48, 46) sts.
Dec 1 st at each end of next and foll 13 (13, 14, 13, 12) alt rows. 20 sts.
Work 1 row straight, then cast off all sts.

Finishing
With RS facing and using 4mm needles, starting at row-ends side of cast-on edge, pick up and knit 220 (240, 270, 280, 300) sts along lower (row-end) edge.
Work 6 rows in Moss Stitch.
Cast off all sts.

Weave in ends, but do not trim. Soak jacket in tepid water for 20 minutes. Squeeze gently and place between towels. Press to remove excess water. Lay a large towel on a flat surface, into which you can pin (carpet or foam tiles work well). Spread out the jacket to measurements and pin out to dry. When completely dry sew sleeve seams and set-in sleeves. Trim all ends.

Measurements

25cm all sizes

34 (36, 39, 42, 45) cm

40 (42, 46, 47.5, 48) cm

78 (78, 80, 82, 82) cm

42 (47, 53, 57, 66) cm

44 (48, 53, 55, 57) cm

30 (30, 31, 33, 33) cm

45 (46, 48, 50.5, 53,) cm

43 (43, 45, 46, 46) cm

34 (36, 38, 40, 42) cm

Cogges hat

by Jeni Hewlett

A hat-full of chunky cables in a colour that zings.

Pattern notes

This speedy project will just fly off your needles – it is knitted flat with just one quick seam to sew up at the end.

Hat

BRIM

Cast on 71 sts using 5.5mm needles.
Row 1 (RS): K1, *P1, K1; rep from * to end.
Row 2 (WS): P1, *K1, P1; rep from * to end.
Last 2 rows set rib. Work a further 8 rows in rib as set.

Change to 6mm needles.
Next row: K2, *K3, M1, [K2, M1] twice; rep from * 8 more times, K6. 98sts.
Next row: Purl.

CABLE PATTERN

Cable pattern is also shown on Chart.
Row 1: K1, *C6F, K6; rep from * to last st, K1.
Row 2: Purl.
Row 3: Knit.
Row 4: Purl.
Row 5: K1, *K6, C6B; rep from * to last st, K1.
Row 6: Purl.
Row 7: Knit.
Row 8: Purl.
These 8 rows set Cable patt. Cont to work in Cable patt until piece meas 18cm from cast-on edge, ending with RS facing for next row.

SHAPE CROWN

Next row (RS): K1, [K2tog] 48 times, K1. 50 sts.
Work 9 more rows in st st.
Next row [RS]: K1, [K2tog] 24 times, K1. 26 sts.
Work 4 more rows in st st.
Next row [WS]: P1, [P2tog] 12 times, P1. 14 sts.
Work 2 more rows in st st.
Next row [RS]: K1, [K2tog] 6 times, K1. 8 sts.
Break yarn, thread through remaining stitches and fasten off.
With right sides held together, seam the two row-end edges.

Soak and block hat firmly over a pudding basin to shape. Weave in all ends.

Skills

Simple cables

Size

To fit adult head, circumference 50-55cm (19½-21 ½in)

Yarn

Fyberspates Scrumptious Chunky (45% silk, 55% merino; 100g skeins) Magenta (205) 1 x 100g skein

Needles and accessories

1 pair 5.5mm (UK 5/US 9) knitting needles
1 pair 6mm (UK 4/US 10) knitting needles
Cable needle (cn)

Tension

20 sts and 28 rows to 10cm over cable pattern using 6mm needles
16 sts and 22 rows to 10cm over st st using 6mm needles

Special abbreviations

C6F: Slip 3 sts to cn and hold at front, K3; K3 from cn
C6B: Slip 3 sts to cn and hold at back, K3; K3 from cn
Standard abbreviations appear on page 71.

Key

- ☐ Knit on RS, Purl on WS
- C6F
- C6B
- ☐ Pattern repeat

Chart

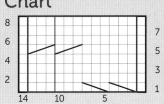

Cogges armwarmers

by Jeni Hewlett

Long cabled armwarmers match the Cogges hat – with optional ribbon trim.

Pattern notes

Trendy long armwarmers in a striking colour, knitted flat with a simple seam to join, and finished with ribbons.

Armwarmers

Make 2 alike

CUFF

Cast on 50 sts.

Row 1 (WS): *K1, P1; rep from * to end of row.

Row 2 (RS): As row 1.

These 2 rows set 1 x 1 rib. Work 3 more rows in 1 x 1 rib, ending with RS facing for next row.

CABLE PATTERN

Cable patt is also shown on Chart.

Row 1 (RS): K1, *C6F, K6; rep from * to last st, K1.

Row 2: Purl.

Row 3: Knit.

Row 4: Purl.

Row 5: K1, *K6, C6B; rep from * to last st, K1.

Row 6: Purl.

Row 7: Knit.

Row 8: Purl.

These 8 rows set Cable patt. Work these 8 rows 8 more times.

DECREASE FOR HAND

Row 1 (RS): *K3, K2tog; rep from * to end. 40 sts.

Row 2: Purl

Row 3: *K2, K2tog; rep from * to end. 30 sts.

Work in 1 x 1 rib as set for cuff, for 5 rows.

Cast off, leaving a tail long enough to seam the armwarmers.

Making up

Soak and block the two pieces by stretching gently to measurements. Wait until they are completely dry. From the cast-off edge, sew a 4cm seam joining the row-end edges of the armwarmer, then leave the next 4cm unseamed to create the thumb-hole. The yarn can then be carried down the open edge, rather than cutting and joining again. Continue the seam down to the cast-on edge of the armwarmer. Weave in all ends.

If desired, thread ribbon just under the rib at the top of the hand, passing it through the centre of the stitches. As the yarn is so chunky there is no need for eyelets. Tie the ribbon in a small bow to secure.

Skills

Simple cables

Size

38cm (15in) long
25cm (10in) arm circumference at cuff

Yarn

Fyberspates Scrumptious Chunky (45% silk, 55% merino; 100g skeins)
Magenta (205) 2 x 100g skeins

Needles and accessories

1 pair 6mm (UK 4/US 10) knitting needles
Cable needle (cn)
Ribbon approx 15mm wide and 120cm long

Tension

20 sts and 28 rows to 10cm over cable pattern using 6mm needles

Special abbreviations

C6F: Slip 3 sts to cn and hold at front, K3; K3 from cn
C6B: Slip 3 sts to cn and hold at back, K3; K3 from cn
Standard abbreviations appear on page 71.

Key

- ☐ Knit on RS, Purl on WS
- ◪ C6F
- ◪ C6B
- ☐ Pattern repeat

Chart

Uffington

by Jeni Hewlett

Leafy lace gives this waistcoat real personality.

Skills
Simple lace

Size

To fit bust

8-10	12-14	16-18	20-22	24-26	
81-86	91-97	102-107	112-117	122-127	cm
32-34	36-38	40-42	44-46	48-50	in

Actual bust

86	97	107	117	127	cm
34	38	42	46	50	in

Actual length

45	48	49	51	53	cm
17½	19	19½	20	21	in

Yarn
Fyberspates Scrumptious Chunky
(45% silk, 55% merino; 100g skeins)
Cherry (200) 4 (4, 5, 6, 6) x 100g
skeins

Needles and accessories
1 pair each 5.5mm (UK 5/US 9)
knitting needles and circular needles
approx 80cm
1 pair 6mm (UK 4/US 10) knitting
needles
4 buttons, approx 22mm

Tension
Single Leaf panel meas 6cm wide on
6mm needles
Double Leaf panel meas 12cm wide
on 6mm needles
16 sts and 22 rows to 10cm over st st
using 6mm needles

Abbreviations
Standard abbreviations appear on
page 71.

Pattern notes
Unless otherwise instructed, work
decreases and increases 1 stitch in
from edge of pieces.

Back
Cast on 75 (83, 91, 99, 107) sts using
5.5mm needles.
Row 1 (RS): *K1, P1; rep from * to last
st, K1.
Row 2 (WS): P1, *K1, P1; rep from *
to end.
These 2 rows set rib. Cont to work in
rib for 6 more rows (8 rows in total).

Change to 6mm needles.
Setup row (RS): K1, M1, K23 (27, 31, 35,
39), P2, K10, P2, K10, P2, K25 (29, 33,
37, 41). 76 (84, 92, 100, 108) sts.
Setup row 2 (WS): P25 (29, 33, 37, 41),
K2, P10, K2, P10, K2, P25 (29, 33, 37, 41).

DOUBLE LEAF PANEL
In the following section the Double
Leaf panel is also shown on the Chart.
Row 1 (RS): K25 (29, 33, 37, 41), P2,
K6, K3tog, yo, K1, yo, P2, yo, K1, yo,
Sl 1, K2tog, psso, K6, P2, K25 (29, 33,
37, 41).
Row 2 and all foll WS rows: P25 (29,
33, 37, 41), K2, P10, K2, P10, K2, P25
(29, 33, 37, 41).
Row 3: K25 (29, 33, 37, 41), P2, K4,
K3tog, K1, yo, K1, yo, K1, P2, K1, yo, K1,
yo, K1, Sl 1, K2tog, psso, K4, P2, K25
(29, 33, 37, 41).
Row 5: K25 (29, 33, 37, 41), P2, K2,
K3tog, K2, yo, K1, yo, K2, P2, K2, yo, K1,
yo, K2, Sl 1, K2tog, psso, K2, P2, K25
(29, 33, 37, 41).
Row 7: K25 (29, 33, 37, 41), P2, K3tog,
K3, yo, K1, yo, K3, P2, K3, yo, K1, yo,
K3, Sl 1, K2tog, psso, P2, K25 (29, 33,
37, 41).
Row 8: As Row 2.
Rows 1 - 8 set st st with Double Leaf
panel.
Cont to work in st st with Double Leaf
panel and, **at the same time**, dec 1 st
at each end of next and 3 foll alt rows.
68 (76, 84, 92, 100) sts.
Work WS row, and then 8 more rows
in patt.

Keeping patts corr as set, inc 1 st at
each end of next and 3 foll alt rows.
76 (84, 92, 100, 108) sts.
Work WS row.
4 leaf patt repeats should now be
complete. Piece should meas approx
19cm.
Work straight in patts as set until piece
meas 26 (28, 28, 29, 30) cm from
cast-on edge, ending with RS facing
for next row.

SHAPE ARMHOLES
Keeping patts corr, cast off 4 (5, 6, 7,
8) sts at start of next two rows. 68 (74,
80, 86, 92) sts.
Dec 1 st at each end of every row 1 (1,
3, 3, 5) times and on foll alt row 1 (2, 1,
2, 2) times, then on 2 foll 4th rows. 60
(64, 68, 72, 74) sts.
Work straight in patt as set until
armhole meas 17 (18, 19, 20, 21) cm,
ending with RS facing for next row.

SHAPE SHOULDERS
Cast off 5 (6, 7, 7, 7) sts at start of next
2 rows. 50 (52, 54, 58, 60) sts.
Cast off 5 (6, 6, 7, 7) sts at start of
next row, then knit until you have 7
(7, 8, 9, 10) sts on RH needle, turn,
leaving remaining 38 (39, 40, 42, 43)
sts on a holder.
Cast off 2 (2, 2, 3, 4) sts at start of next
row and purl to end.
Cast off rem 5 (5, 6, 6, 6) sts.

Place centre 26 sts on a holder for
back neck.
With RS facing, rejoin yarn to rem 12
(13, 14, 16, 17) sts and knit to end.
Cast off 5 (6, 6, 7, 7) sts at start of next
row, and purl to end. 7 (7, 8, 9, 10) sts.
Cast off 2 (2, 2, 3, 4) sts and knit to
end.
Cast off rem 5 (5, 6, 6, 6) sts.

Left Front
Cast on 37 (41, 45, 49, 53) sts using
5.5mm needles.
Row 1 (RS): *K1, P1; rep from * to last
st, K1.
Row 2 (WS): P1, *K1, P1; rep from *
to end.

Uffington continued

These 2 rows set rib. Cont to work in rib for 6 more rows (8 rows in total). Change to 6mm needles.
Setup row (RS): K1, M1, K23 (27, 31, 35, 39), P2, K10, P1. 38 (42, 46, 50, 54) sts.
Setup row 2 (WS): K1, P10, K2, P25 (29, 33, 37, 41).

LEFT SINGLE LEAF PANEL
In the following section the Left Single Leaf panel is also shown on the chart.
Row 1 (RS): K25 (29, 33, 37, 41), P2, K6, K3tog, yo, K1, yo, P1.
Row 2 and all foll WS rows: K1, P10, K2, P25 (29, 33, 37, 41).
Row 3: K25 (29, 33, 37, 41), P2, K4, K3tog, K1, yo, K1, yo, K1, P1.
Row 5: K25 (29, 33, 37, 41), P2, K2, K3tog, K2, yo, K1, yo, K2, P1.
Row 7: K25 (29, 33, 37, 41), P2, K3tog, K3, yo, K1, yo, K3, P1.
Row 8: As row 2.
These 8 rows set st st with Left Single Leaf panel.
Cont to work in st st with Left Single Leaf panel, and at the same time, dec 1 st at start of next and 3 foll alt rows. 34 (38, 42, 46, 50) sts.
Work WS row, and then 8 more rows in patt.
Keeping patts corr as set, inc 1 st at each end of next and 3 foll alt rows. 38 (42, 46, 50, 54) sts.
Work WS row.
4 leaf patt repeats should now be complete. Piece should meas approx 19cm.
Work straight in patts as set until piece meas 26 (28, 28, 29, 30) cm from cast-on edge, ending with RS facing for next row.

SHAPE ARMHOLES
Cast off 4 (5, 6, 7, 8) sts at start of next row. 34 (37, 40, 43, 46) sts.
Work 1 row straight.
Dec 1 st at start of every row 1 (1, 3, 3, 5) times and on foll alt row 1 (2, 1, 2, 2) times, then on 2 foll 4th rows. 30 (32, 34, 36, 37) sts.
Work 1 row straight in patt, ending with RS facing for next row.

SHAPE NECK
Knit to last 15 (15, 15, 16, 17) sts, turn leaving rem sts on a holder for front neck.
Work straight in st st as set until armhole meas 17 (18, 19, 20, 21) cm, ending with RS facing for next row. 15 (17, 19, 20, 20) sts.

SHAPE SHOULDERS
Cast off 5 (6, 7, 7, 7) sts at start of next row. 10 (11, 12, 13, 13) sts.
Work 1 row straight.
Cast off 5 (6, 6, 7, 7) sts at start of next row and cast off rem 5 (5, 6, 6, 6) sts on foll alt row.

Right Front
Cast on 37 (41, 45, 49, 53) sts using 5.5mm needles.
Row 1 (RS): *K1, P1; rep from * to last st, K1.
Row 2 (WS): P1, *K1, P1; rep from * to end.
These 2 rows set rib. Cont to work in rib for 6 more rows (8 rows in total).

Change to 6mm needles.
Setup row (RS): P1, K10, P2, K23 (27, 31, 35, 39), M1, K1. 38 (42, 46, 50, 54) sts.
Setup row 2 (WS): P25 (29, 33, 37, 41), K2, P10, K1.

RIGHT SINGLE LEAF PANEL
In the following section the Right Single Leaf panel is also shown on the Chart.
Row 1 (RS): P1, yo, K1, yo, Sl 1, K2tog, psso, K6, P2, K25 (29, 33, 37, 41).
Row 2 and all foll WS rows: P25 (29, 33, 37, 41), K2, P10, K1.
Row 3: P1, K1, yo, K1, yo, K1, Sl 1, K2tog, psso, K4, P2, K25 (29, 33, 37, 41).
Row 5: P1, K2, yo, K1, yo, K2, Sl 1, K2tog, psso, K2, P2, K25 (29, 33, 37, 41).
Row 7: P1, K3, yo, K1, yo, K3, Sl 1, K2tog, psso, P2, K25 (29, 33, 37, 41).
Row 8: As row 2.
These 8 rows set st st with Right Single Leaf panel.
Cont to work in st st with Right Single Leaf panel and, **at the same time**, dec 1 st at end of next and 3 foll alt rows. 34 (38, 42, 46, 50) sts.
Work WS row, and then 8 more rows in patt.
Keeping patts corr as set, inc 1 st at end of next and 3 foll alt rows. 38 (42, 46, 50, 54) sts.
Work WS row.
4 leaf patt repeats should now be complete. Piece should meas approx 19cm.
Work straight in patts as set until piece meas 26 (28, 28, 29, 30) cm from cast-on edge, ending with WS facing for next row.

SHAPE ARMHOLES
Cast off 4 (5, 6, 7, 8) sts at start of next row. 34 (37, 40, 43, 46) sts.
Dec 1 st at end of every row 1 (1, 3, 3, 5) times and on foll alt row 1 (2, 1, 2, 2) times, then on 2 foll 4th rows. 30 (32, 34, 36, 37) sts.

SHAPE NECK
Next row (WS): Purl to last 15 (15, 15, 16, 17) sts, and leave these 15 (15, 15, 16, 17) sts on a holder for front neck.
Work straight in st st as set until armhole meas 17 (18, 19, 20, 21) cm, ending with WS facing for next row. 15 (17, 19, 20, 20) sts.

SHAPE SHOULDERS
Cast off 5 (6, 7, 7, 7) sts at start of next row. 10 (11, 12, 13, 13) sts.
Work 1 row straight.
Cast off 5 (6, 6, 7, 7) sts at start of next row and cast off rem 5 (5, 6, 6, 6) sts on foll alt row.

Making up
Weave in ends, but do not trim. Soak pieces in tepid water for 20 minutes. Squeeze gently and place between towels. Press to remove excess water. Lay a large towel on a flat surface, into which you can pin (carpet or foam tiles work well). Spread out the pieces to measurements and pin out to dry.
Join side and shoulder seams.

NECKBAND
Using 5.5mm circular needles, with RS facing and starting at sts on holder for Right Front neck, knit 15 (15, 15, 16, 17) from holder, pick up and knit 20 (20, 22, 22, 24) sts up right neck edge, pick up and knit 2 (2, 2, 3, 4) sts from right back neck and knit 26 sts from holder for back neck decreasing 1 st in centre, pick up and knit 2 (2, 2, 3, 4) sts from Left Back neck, pick up and knit 20 (20, 22, 22, 24) sts down left neck edge and knit 15 (15, 15, 16, 17) sts from holder for front neck. 99 (99, 103, 107, 115) sts.
Row 1 (WS): [P1, K1] 6 (6, 6, 7, 7) times, P1, K3tog, [P1, K1] 33 (33, 35, 35, 39) times, P1, K3tog, P1, [K1, P1] 6 (6, 6, 7, 7) times. 95 (95, 99, 103, 111) sts.
Row 2 (RS): *K1, P1; rep from * to last st, K1.
Row 3: Rib 12 (12, 12, 14, 14), K3tog, rib to last 15 (15, 15, 17, 17) sts, K3tog, rib to end. 91 (91, 95, 99, 107) sts.

Row 4: Work in rib as set.
Row 5: Rib 11 (11, 11, 13, 13), K3tog, rib to last 14 (14, 14, 16, 16) sts, K3tog, rib to end. 87 (87, 91, 95, 103) sts.
Row 6: As row 4.
Row 7: Rib 10 (10, 10, 12, 12), K3tog, rib to last 13 (13, 13, 15, 15) sts, K3tog, rib to end. 83 (83, 87, 91, 99) sts.
Cast off in rib.

BUTTON BAND

Using 5.5mm needles, with RS facing and starting at top of left neck band, pick up and knit 5 sts from edge of neck band, then pick up and knit 50 (56, 56, 58, 60) sts evenly down front edge. 55 (61, 61, 63, 65) sts.
Row 1 (WS): *P1, K1; rep from * to last st, P1.
Row 2 (RS): *K1, P1; rep from * to last st, K1.
These two rows set rib. Work a further 5 rows in rib as set.
Cast off in rib.

BUTTONHOLE BAND

Using 5.5mm needles, with RS facing, and starting at bottom of right front edge, pick up and knit 50 (56, 56, 58, 60) sts evenly to start of neck, then pick up and knit 5 sts from edge of neck band. 55 (61, 61, 63, 65) sts.
Row 1 (WS): *P1, K1; rep from * to last st, P1.
Row 2 (RS): *K1, P1; rep from * to last st, K1.
Row 3: As row 1.
Row 4: [K1, P1] 1 (1, 1, 2, 2) times, K1, *yo, K2tog, [P1, K1] 7 (8, 8, 8, 8) times; rep from * twice more, yo, K2tog, [P1, K1] 1 (1, 1, 1, 2) times.
Rows 5-7: Work in rib as set.
Cast off in rib.

ARMBANDS

Using 5.5mm circular needles, with RS facing, and starting in centre of underarm, pick up and knit 62 (66, 72, 76, 82) sts evenly round armhole. Join to work in the round and place marker for start of round.
Round 1: *K1, P1; rep from * to end of round.
Repeat last round 6 more times.
Cast off in rib. Repeat for other armhole.

Sew buttons to button band to match buttonholes.
Weave in all ends.

Key

	Knit on RS, Purl on WS
●	Purl on RS, Knit on WS
⅄	Sl 1, K2tog, psso
O	Yarnover
⅄	K3tog

Chart

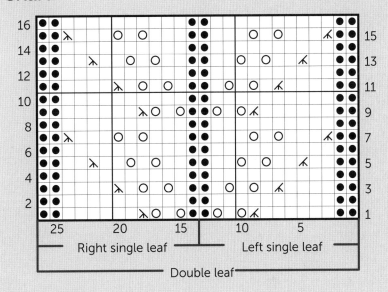

Measurements

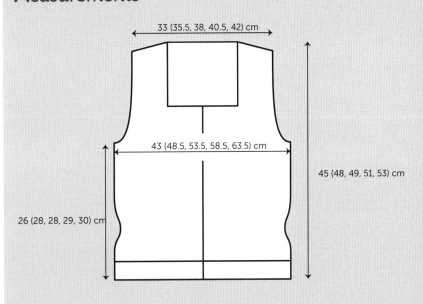

Alvescot

by Jeni Hewlett

Elegant lace panels accentuate this fitted sweater.

Skills

Lace patterns, shaping in lace

Size

To fit bust

8	10	12	14	16	18	20	22	
81	**86**	**91**	**97**	**102**	**107**	**112**	**117**	cm
32	34	36	38	40	42	44	46	in

Actual bust

86	**91**	**97**	**102**	**107**	**112**	**117**	**122**	cm
34	36	38	40	42	44	46	48	in

Actual length

53	**55**	**55**	**55**	**56**	**58**	**58**	**60**	cm
21	21½	21½	21½	22	23	23	23	in

Sleeve seam

45	**45**	**46**	**47**	**47**	**47**	**47**	**47**	cm
17½	17½	18	18½	18½	18½	18½	18½	in

Yarn

Fyberspates Scrumptious Chunky (45% silk, 55% merino; 100g skeins)
Biscuit (203) 8 (8, 9, 9, 10, 10, 11, 11) x 100g skeins

Needles and accessories

1 pair 6mm (UK 4/US 10) knitting needles
1 set 6mm (UK 4/US 10) circular needles, 60cm long
Cable needle (cn), stitch markers

Tension

17 sts and 21 rows to 10cm in lace and cable patt using 6mm needles

Special abbreviations

C4F: Sl 2 sts to cn, hold at front, K2; K2 from cn
C4B: Sl 2 sts to cn, hold at back, K2; K2 from cn
C2F: Sl 1 st to cn, hold at front, K1; K1 from cn
C2B: Sl 1 st to cn, hold at back, K1; K1 from cn

Stitch patterns

LACE PATTERN FOR BODY

This pattern is worked between markers on the Body. Chart A also shows this pattern.

Row 1 (RS) : K1, yo, K2tog, K2, yo, SSK, K2, yo, SSK, P2, yo, K4, SSK, K6, K2tog, K4, yo, P2, K2, yo, SSK, K4, SSK, yo, K1.
Row 2: P4, K1, yo, P2tog, P2, yo, P2tog, K2, P1, yo, P4, P2tog, P4, P2tog tbl, P4, yo, P1, K2, P2, yo, P2tog, P2, K1, P4.
Row 3: K5, yo, SSK, K2, yo, SSK, P2, K2, yo, K4, SSK, K2, K2tog, K4, yo, K2, P2, K2, yo, SSK, K7.
Row 4: P4, K1, yo, P2tog, P2, yo, P2tog, K2, P3, yo, P4, P2tog, P2tog tbl, P4, yo, P3, K2, P2, yo, P2tog, P2, K1, P4.
Rows 5-12: Rep rows 1 to 4 twice.
Row 13: K1, yo, K2tog, K5, K2tog, K4, yo, P2, [K2, yo, SSK] 3 times, P2, yo, K4, SSK, K5, SSK, yo, K1.
Row 14: P4, K1, P2, P2tog tbl, P4, yo, P1, K2, [P2, yo, P2tog] 3 times, K2, P1, yo, P4, P2tog, P2, K1, P4.
Row 15: K6, K2tog, K4, yo, K2, P2, [K2, yo, SSK] 3 times, P2, K2, yo, K4, SSK, K6.
Row 16: P4, K1, P2tog tbl, P4, yo, P3, K2, [P2, yo, P2tog] 3 times, K2, P3, yo, P4, P2tog, K1, P4.
Rows 17-24: Rep rows 13-16 twice.
Repeat rows 1-24 as necessary.

LACE PATTERN FOR SLEEVES

Chart B shows lace stitch pattern for the sleeves.
Row 1: K1, yo, K4, SSK, K6, K2tog, K4, yo, K1.
Row 2: K1, P1, yo, P4, P2tog, P4, P2tog tbl, P4, yo, P1, K1.
Row 3: K3, yo, K4, SSK, K2, K2tog, K4, yo, K3.
Row 4: K1, P3, yo, P4, P2tog, P2tog tbl, P4, yo, P3, K1.
Repeat rows 1-4 as necessary.

Pattern notes

Lace pattern is worked on RS and WS rows. If you are new to lace, consider using stitch markers between lace sections and count sts in lace sections at the end of every row.

Back

Cast on 74 (78, 82, 86, 90, 94, 98, 102) sts.
Size 8
Row 1: K1, [P2, K4] twice, P2, pm, Row 1 of lace patt, pm, [P2, K4] 2 times, P2, K1.
Size 10
Row 1: K1, P2, [K4, P3] twice, pm, Row 1 of lace patt, pm, [P3, K4] twice, P2, K1.
Size 12
Row 1: K1, P1, K4, [P2, K4] twice, P1, pm, Row 1 of lace patt, pm, P1, [K4, P2] twice, K4, P1, K1.
Size 14
Row 1: K1, [P2, K4] 3 times, P2, pm, Row 1 of lace patt, pm, [P2, K4] 3 times, P2, K1.
Size 16
Row 1: K1, [P3, K4] twice, P2, K4, P2, pm, Row 1 of lace patt, pm, P2, K4, P2, [K4, P3] twice, K1.
Size 18
Row 1: K1, [P3, K4] 3 times, P3, pm, Row 1 of lace patt, pm, P3, [K4, P3] 3 times, K1.
Size 20
Row 1: K1, [P2, K4] 4 times, P2, pm, Row 1 of lace patt, pm, [P2, K4] 4 times, P2, K1.
Size 22
Row 1: K1, P1, K4, [P3, K4] 3 times, P2, pm, Row 1 of lace patt, pm, P2, [K4, P3] 3 times, K4, P1, K1.
All sizes
Row 2 (WS): Work to marker in rib as set in row 1, slm, Row 2 of lace patt, slm, work to end in rib as set by previous row.
Row 3: Work in rib as set, but C4B instead of each K4, slm, Row 3 of lace patt, slm, work in rib as set, but C4F instead of each K4.
Row 4: Work in rib as set, slm, Row 4 of lace patt, slm, work in rib as set.

Row 5: Work as set, but C4B instead of each K4, slm, Row 5 of lace patt, slm, work as set, but C4F instead of each K4.

Continue to work in rib and lace pattern as set, with cables on each RS row, until row 24 has been worked. Repeat rows 1-24, with cables on all RS rows, until work meas 32 (33, 33, 33, 33, 34.5, 34.5, 34.5) cm or until desired length to underarm.

SHAPE ARMHOLES

Keeping patt corr, cast off 3 (3, 4, 4, 4, 4, 4, 4) sts at the beg of the next 2 rows. 68 (72, 74, 78, 82, 86, 90, 94) sts. Then cast off 1 (2, 2, 2, 2, 2, 2, 2) sts at the beg of the next 10 (6, 6, 8, 10, 10, 10, 10) rows. 58 (60, 62, 62, 62, 66, 70, 74) sts.

Size 22 only
Cast off 1 st at the start of the next 2 rows. 72 sts.

All sizes
***Continue in pattern without shaping until work measures 18.5 (19, 19.5, 19.5, 20.5, 20.5, 21, 21) cm from the initial underarm cast off.

SHAPE SHOULDERS

Loosely cast off 5 (6, 6, 6, 6, 6, 6, 7) sts at beg of the next 6 rows. 28 (24, 26, 26, 26, 30, 34, 30) sts. Loosely cast off the rem sts.

Front

Work as for Back until ***.
Cont in patt without shaping until piece meas 6 rows less than Back to start of shoulder shaping, ending with RS facing for next row.

SHAPE NECK

Next row (RS): Work 25 (26, 27, 27, 27, 28, 29, 30) sts in patt and put these sts just worked on a st holder, cast off next 8 (8, 8, 8, 8, 10, 12, 12) sts, work rem sts in patt.
§ Work one row.
Row 1: At the neck edge, cast off 3 (2, 3, 3, 3, 2, 3, 3) sts.
Row 2: Work without shaping.
Row 3: At the neck edge, cast off 2 (2, 2, 2, 2, 2, 3, 2) sts.
Row 4: Work without shaping.
Row 5: At the neck edge, cast off 2 (2, 2, 2, 2, 2, 2, 2) sts.
Row 6: At the shoulder edge, cast off 5 (6, 6, 6, 6, 6, 6, 7) sts.
Row 7: At the neck edge, cast off 2 (1, 1, 1, 1, 2, 2, 1) sts.

Chart A: Body Lace

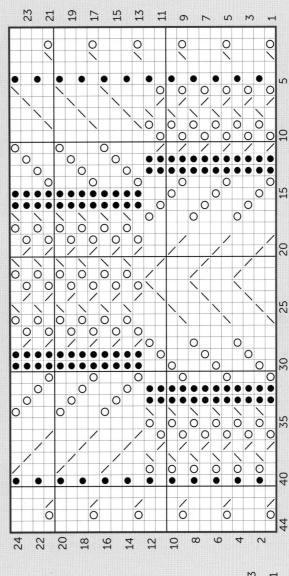

Key

☐	Knit on RS, Purl on WS
●	Purl on RS, Knit on WS
╱	SSK on RS, P2tog tbl on WS
╲	K2tog on RS, P2tog on WS
○	Yarnover
☐	Pattern repeat

Chart B: Sleeves

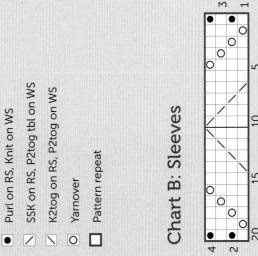

Row 8: At the shoulder edge, cast off 5 (6, 6, 6, 6, 6, 6, 7) sts.

Row 9: At the neck edge, cast off 1 (1, 1, 1, 1, 2, 1, 1) st.

Row 10: At the shoulder edge, cast off final 5 (6, 6, 6, 6, 6, 6, 7) sts.
Break yarn.
With RS facing, rejoin yarn at armhole edge of Left Front shoulder and work from § to complete shoulder.

Sleeves

Make 2 alike

Cast on 34 (34, 34, 36, 36, 38, 40, 40) sts.

Sizes 8-12

Row 1: P1, K4, P2, pm, Row 1 of sleeve lace patt, pm, P2, K4, P1.

Sizes 14-16

Row 1: P2, K4, P2, pm, Row 1 of sleeve lace patt, pm, P2, K4, P2.

Size 18

Row 1: K1, P2, K4, P2, pm, Row 1 of sleeve lace patt, pm, P2, K4, P2, K1.

Sizes 20-22

Row 1: K2, P2, K4, P2, pm, Row 1 of sleeve lace patt, pm, P2, K4, P2, K2.

All sizes

Row 2 (WS): Work to marker in rib as set, slm, Row 2 of sleeve lace patt, work in rib as set to end of row.

Row 3: Work to marker in rib as set, slm, Row 3 of sleeve lace patt, slm, work in rib as set, to end of row.

Row 4: Work to marker as set, slm, Row 4 of sleeve lace patt, slm, work as set to end.

The following sleeve increases should be incorporated into a 2x2 rib on each side of the sleeve – working a C2B before the lace patt and C2F after the lace patt when working cable rows. Repeat rows 5-8 (as below), increasing one st at each end of every 6th (6th, 6th, 6th, 4th, 4th, 4th, 4th) row until 58 (60, 62, 64, 70, 72, 76, 80) sts.

Row 5: Work to marker as set, but C4B instead of K4 and C2B instead of K2, slm, row 1 of sleeve lace patt, slm, work as set, but C4F instead of K4 and C2F instead of K2.

Row 6: Work to marker in rib as set, slm, Row 2 of sleeve lace patt, slm, work as set to end.

Row 7: Work to marker as set, but C4B instead of K4 and C2B instead of K2, slm, Row 3 of sleeve lace patt, slm, work as set, but C4F instead of K4 and C2F instead of K2, to end of row.

Row 8: Work to marker in rib as set, slm, Row 4 of sleeve lace patt, slm, work in rib as set to end.
Cont in patt until piece meas 45 (45, 46, 47, 47, 47, 47, 47) cm, or until desired length.

SHAPE SLEEVEHEAD

Keeping patt corr, cast off 4 (4, 5, 5, 5, 5, 5, 5) sts at beg of the next 2 rows. 50 (52, 52, 54, 60, 62, 66, 70) sts.
Dec 1 st each end of every other row (one st in from the edge), 13 (14, 10, 11, 14, 15, 17, 19) times.
24 (24, 32, 32, 32, 32, 32, 32) sts.
Cast off 3 (3, 4, 4, 4, 4, 4, 4) sts at the start of the next 4 rows. Cast off rem 12 (12, 16, 16, 16, 16, 16, 16) sts.

Making up

Weave in ends but do not trim. Soak pieces in tepid water for 20 minutes. Squeeze gently and place between towels. Press to remove excess water. Lay a large towel on a flat surface, into which you can pin (carpet or foam tiles work well). Spread out the pieces to measurements and pin out to dry. When completely dry, unpin and trim ends.
Sew shoulder seams.
Set in sleeves and sew sleeve and side seams.

Collar

Beg at the left shoulder seam, using 6mm circular needle, pick up and knit sts around neck as folls:
16 (16, 17, 17, 17, 18, 18, 18) sts down left front edge, 10 (10, 11, 11, 11, 12, 12, 12) sts across front neck, 16 (16, 17, 17, 17, 18, 18, 18) sts up right front edge, 42 (42, 45, 45, 45, 48, 48, 48) sts across back neck. 84 (84, 90, 90, 90, 96, 96, 96) sts.
The cables on the collar are worked on the inside, so they will show correctly when the collar is worn folded down.

Row 1: *P2, K4; rep from * to end.

Row 2: *K2, P4; rep from * to end.

Row 3: *P2, C4B; rep from * to end.
Repeat rows 2 and 3 until collar meas 15cm, or to the desired length.
Cast off.

Sew collar seam and weave in all ends.

Measurements

43 (45.5, 48.5, 51, 53.5, 56, 58.5, 61) cm

45 (45, 46, 47, 47, 47, 47, 47) cm

32 (33, 33, 33, 34.5, 34.5, 34.5) cm

53 (55, 55, 55, 56, 58, 58, 58) cm

information

Techniques and advice

Tension

Obtaining the correct tension (US: gauge) for all stitch patterns is vital to achieving the correct results for your knitted item. The needle sizes given are only suggestions. Every knitter is different, and the fact that your tension matches in one pattern does not guarantee that it will match in another. Always knit a good-sized swatch, around 15cm square is ideal. Where tension information is given for a pattern repeat, add 5 to 10 sts in garter stitch at each end of the rows, so that you aren't measuring distorted edge stitches.

Having knitted your swatch, it is also vital to soak it in tepid water and pin it out to dry, stretching it out as you intend to stretch the finished item. For lace patterns, the swatch should be pinned out hard and for other patterns it should just be smoothed out gently.

Once your swatch is dry, unpin it and measure carefully the number of stitches and rows over the central 10cm. If you have the correct number of stitches and rows, you are using the correct sized needles. If you have too many stitches (and rows), you will need to knit another swatch with larger needles. If you have too few stitches (and rows), you will need to try smaller needles. It is really important to match the tension given in all stitch patterns; the needle size that you use to do this does not matter. It is the tension that determines the finished size of your pieces, how much yarn is used and whether the pieces will fit together as intended.

Sizing

The garments in this book have been designed with different amounts of ease. Positive ease is when the actual garment is larger than the body measurements and negative ease is when the actual garment is smaller than the body measurements. Knitwear is inherently stretchy, so to ensure a fitted look for garments with negative ease, choose the size with "To fit" measurements closest to your body measurements. If you want a less fitted finish, then do choose a larger size.

Where there is only one set of numbers in a pattern instruction, it refers to all sizes. When more than one number is given, the smallest size appears first, with the larger sizes appearing inside brackets in size order. It is always useful to circle or highlight the size you are working throughout the pattern before you start. Read the pattern carefully, as sometimes smaller groups of sizes are treated separately. It is always marked clearly where the instructions return to all sizes.

Each garment also includes a diagram showing actual final measurements that will help you to decide which size you need to knit. Where helpful, these diagrams also include grey arrows to show the direction of knitting.

Shaping in lace

Lace patterns rely on combinations of increases (usually yarn overs) and decreases to create an open or lace pattern. When the pattern instructions say to work shaping while keeping a lace pattern correct, it is important to only work lace increases (or decreases) if you will have enough stitches to work the corresponding lace decreases (or increases). Where it is not possible to do this, the relevant stitches should be replaced with stocking stitch. If you are unsure, replace the whole of the affected lace repeat with stocking stitch.

Using charts

Charts are a graphical representation of your knitting, with each square representing a stitch (or small group of stitches) and every row of squares representing a row or round of knitting. Charts for designs that are knitted back and forth are read from right to left for RS rows (usually odd numbered rows) and from left to right for WS rows (usually even numbered rows). Some charts start on a WS row and these are clearly noted on the chart pages. In these cases odd numbered rows are WS and even numbered rows are RS. For designs that are knitted in the round, all chart rows are read from right to left. This article from Knitty.com is a helpful tutorial on knitting from charts: www.tinyurl.com/KnittingCharts

Techniques used

BOOKS

A good general knitting techniques book will be invaluable for helping you with some of the methods used in this book. We would recommend the following books:

The Knitting Answer Book by Margaret Radcliffe. ISBN 978-0715325759

Knitting Without Tears by Elizabeth Zimmermann. ISBN 978-0684135052

ONLINE TUTORIALS

The internet is a great source of helpful tutorials and techniques videos. Here are a few of our favourites:

Grafting (Kitchener stitch) is covered in this article from Knitty.com: www.tinyurl.com/KitchenerStitch

Short-row shaping is shown in this video from KnittingHelp.com: www.tinyurl.com/ShortRowShaping

Folded hems are explained on Marnie MacLean's blog: www.tinyurl.com/FoldedHems

Knitted pleats are covered on the Crafty Diversions Blog: www.tinyurl.com/KnittedPleats

The cable, long-tail and provisional cast-on methods are all covered by videos at KnittingHelp.com: www.tinyurl.com/CastOnMethods

Blocking and finishing

Instructions are given within each pattern for how to prepare the knitted pieces for seaming (if required). Do take time to block your work prior to seaming, as it really does make the job easier and the finished garment tidier. Blocking simply involves soaking the knitting for around 20 minutes in tepid water. The piece is then gently squeezed between towels (do not wring out) to remove excess water, before being pinned out to dry. Most garments simply need to be gently smoothed out and shaped with your hands, to make the knitting lie flat, however, lace work will need to be stretched out more firmly to allow the pattern to show up. You may find it helpful to use stainless steel wires as well as pins in these cases, in order to keep straight edges straight.

Seams should be sewn using mattress stitch or a small back stitch if preferred.

Care instructions

With the exception of Scrumptious 4ply/Sport, the Scrumptious yarns are hand wash only. Use tepid water, and follow the blocking instructions above, each time you wash your garment.

Scrumptious 4ply/Sport is machine washable at 40C on a gentle cycle. You will need to follow the same blocking process after each wash.

Previously published

The following patterns included in this book were published previously:
Alvescot (Graceful in *The Knitter* Issue 10)
Cogges armwarmers (Heepy cabled fingerless mittens by Fyberspates)
Wytham (Ostrich Lace Cardigan by Fyberspates)
Challow (Nessa in *The Knitter* Issue 27)

Pattern queries

If you think there may be an error with any of the pattern instructions, please email fyberspates@btinternet.com or call +44 (0)7540 656660.

Scrumptious stockists

UK

Addicted 2 Knitting
Rosemont, Hanney Road, Southmoor, Oxfordshire, OX13 5HT
www.addicted2knitting.co.uk

A Good Yarn
53 Cambridge Street, Cleethorpes, Lincolnshire, DN35 8HD
www.agoodyarn.co.uk

Along Came Polly
22 Westward Rd, Stroud, Gloucestershire, GL5 4JQ

Arty Crafty in Godalming
9 Church Street, Godalming, Surrey, GU7 1EQ
www.artycrafty.com

Baa Ram Ewe
87 Otley Road, Headingley, West Yorkshire, LS6 3PS
www.baaramewe.co.uk

Battle Wool and Needlecraft
2 Mount Street, Battle, East Sussex, TN33 0EG
www.battlewoolshop.co.uk

Beckside Yarns and Needlecrafts
Beckside Gallery, Church Avenue, Clapham, North Yorkshire, LA2 8EA
www.becksideyarns.co.uk

Bodkins
71 Hart Rd, Thundersley, Essex, SS7 3PB
www.bodkins71.co.uk

Creative Yarns and Needlecrafts
18 High Street, Totnes, Devon, TQ9 5RY
www.creative-crafts-needlework.co.uk

Claris's Tea room and Gift Shop
1-3 High Street, Biddenden, Kent, TN27 8AL
www.collectablegifts.net

The Crochet Chain
6-7 Arlington Mews, Waltham Abbey, Essex, EN9 1ED
www.thecrochetchain.co.uk

Darnit and Stitch
Blue Boar Street, Oxford, OX1 1DL
www.darnitandstitch.com

Dancing Hens
Battlers Green Farm, Common Lane, Radlett, Hertfordshire, WD7 8PH

Fabric8
12 Head Street, Colchester, Essex, CO1 1NY
www.fabric8online.co.uk

First4yarns
20 High Street, Knighton, Powys, LD7 1AT
www.first4yarns.co.uk

Five Valleys Designs @ The Style List
13, Market Place, Berkeley, Gloucestershire, GL13 9BP

The Fluff-a-torium
20 West Street, Dorking, Surrey, RH4 1BL

Heavenly Yarns
137 Fore Street, Exeter, Devon, EX4 3AN
www.heavenlyyarns.co.uk

Hulu Crafts
www.hulucrafts.co.uk

Iknit London
106 Lower Marsh, London, SE1 7AB
www.iknitshop.org.uk

Interknit Cafe
60 Downing Street, Farnham, Surrey, GU9 7PN
www.interknitcafe.co.uk

Ippikin
59 High Street, Much Wenlock, Shropshire, TF13 6AE

Jane's Wool Shop
1 New Broadway, Hampton Rd, Hampton Hill, Middlesex, TW12 IJQ

Knitting Parlour
12 Graham Road, Gt Malvern, Worcestershire, WR14 2HN
www.theknittingparlour.co.uk

Knitting Village
The Lodge, Warren Lane, Cottered, Hertfordshire, SG9 9QG
www.knittingvillage.com

Knit Working
5 Main Road, Gedling, Nottingham, NG4 3HQ

Laughing Hens
The Croft Stables, Station Lane, Great Barrow, Cheshire, CH3 7JN
www.laughinghens.com

Scrumptious stockists

Les Tricoteuses
12 Chapel Yard, Albert Street, Holt,
Norfolk, NR25 6HG
www.lestricoteuses.co.uk

Mandors Fabric Store
34 Renfrew Street, Glasgow, G3 6ST
www.mandors.co.uk

Manfield Crafts
24 Griffith Street, Rushden,
Northamptonshire, NN10 0NG
www.manfieldcrafts.com

Marmalade Yarns
11 Catherine Hill, Frome, BA11 4JA
www.marmaladeyarns.co.uk

Meadow Yarns
Castle Meadow New Barn, Bramfield,
Suffolk, IP19 9AJ
www.meadowyarns.co.uk

MoonStone Yarns
Unit D, The Old Waterfall Shopping
Village, Faldo Rd, Barton le Play,
Buckinghamshire, MK45 4RF
www.moonstoneyarns.co.uk

Mrs Moon
41 Crown Rd, Twickenham, Middlesex,
TW1 3EJ
www.mrsmoon.co.uk

Nest
102 Weston Park, Crouch End,
London, N8 9PP
www.handmadenest.co.uk

Pure Purl
www.purepurl.com

Purl City Yarns
62 Port Street, Manchester, M1 2EQ
www.purlcityyarns.com

Purlescence
www.purlescence.co.uk

Tall Yarns
www.tallyarns.co.uk

Tangled Yarn
100 Compstall Road, Romiley,
Stockport, Cheshire, SK6 4DE

Three Bags Full
Unit 3, The Piece Hall, Halifax,
Yorkshire, HX1 1RE

Twist
1 Market Hill, Woodbridge, Suffolk,
IP12 4LP

Twist Yarns in Essex
www.twistyarns.co.uk

We Three
16 Crown Street, Brentwood, Essex,
CM14 4BA

Wool
19 Old Orchard Street, Bath, Somerset,
BA1 1JU
www.woolbath.co.uk

The Wool Bar
15 Warwick Street, Worthing, West
Sussex, BN11 3DF

Woolfish
St Abbs, Berwickshire, Scotland,
TD14 5QF
www.woolfish.co.uk

Yarn Gathering of Stone
2b Radford Street, Stone, ST15 8DA

Yarnspiration
www.yarnspiration.co.uk

EUROPE
Secret wool – Finland
www.secretwool.com

Sarl Distrilaine – France
7 Rue de la Cote d'Or, 44300 Nantes,
France
www.laine-et-tricot.com

Die Wollbox – Germany
www.wollbox.de

Mamamia Kft – Hungary
Mamamia Kft, Fadrusz utca 12,
Budapest, 1114, Hungary

Silki.is – Iceland
Svöluási 7, Reykjavik, Hafnarfirdi, 221,
Iceland

WOOOL – Netherlands
Westeinde 61, 2512 GV Den Haag,
Netherlands
www.wooool.nl

Zagroda – Poland
www.zagroda.co

Garnkorgen – Sweden
www.garnkorgen.se

Galenigarn – Sweden
www.galenigarn.se

**Distributor for Norway and
Denmark:**
Fancy Knit Danmark
Hovedvejen 71, 8586, Ørum Djurs,
Denmark
www.fancyknitdanmark.com

USA
US distributor of Scrumptious yarns:

Knitcellaneous
120 Acorn St, Merlin, OR 97532, USA
Tel: 541 955 9348
www.knitcellaneous.com

REST OF THE WORLD
A Chronic Yarnoholic – Australia
Brisbane, Australia
Email: chronicyarnoholic@yahoo.
com.au

**Holland Road Yarn Company –
New Zealand**
281 Jackson Street, Petone,
Wellington, New Zealand
www.hollandroadyarn.co.nz

Standard abbreviations

alt	alternate
approx	approximately
beg	beginning
C4B	slip 2 sts to cable needle and hold at back, K2; K2 from cable needle
C4F	slip 2 sts to cable needle and hold at front, K2; K2 from cable needle
chst	chain stitch (crochet)
cm	centimetres
cn	cable needle
cont	continue
corr	correct
dc	double crochet (US: single crochet)
dec	decrease/decreasing
DK	double knitting
DPN	double-pointed needle
est	established
foll	follows/following
g	grams
g st	garter stitch (knit every row)
in	inches
inc	increase/increasing
K	knit
K2tog	knit the next two stitches together
KFB	knit into the front and back of the same stitch
kwise	knitwise
LH	left hand
M1	make 1 – as M1L
M1L	make 1 left – pick up the strand between stitches from front to back and knit through the back of this loop
M1LP	make 1 purlwise – pick up the strand between stitches from front to back and purl through the back of this loop
M1R	make 1 right – pick up the strand between stitches from back to front and knit this loop
M1RP	make 1 right purlwise – pick up the strand between stitches from back to front and purl this loop
MB	make a bobble (see pattern for specific instruction)
meas	measures
mm	millimetres

P	purl
p2sso	pass two slipped stitches over
P2tog	purl two stitches together
P3tog	purl three stitches together
patt rep(s)	pattern repeat(s)
patt(s)	pattern(s)
PFB	purl into the front and back of the same stitch
pm	place marker
prev	previous
psso	pass slipped stitch over
pwise	purlwise
rem	remain/remaining
rep(s)	repeat(s)
rev	reverse
rev st st	reverse stocking stitch
RH	right hand
RS	right side
sk2po	slip one stitch knitwise, knit two stitches together, pass slipped stitch over
Sl 1	slip one stitch
slm	slip marker
SSK	slip two stitches knitwise one at a time, knit two slipped stitches together through back of loop
SSP	slip two stitches knitwise one at a time, purl two slipped stitches together through the back of the loops
st st	stocking stitch (US: stockinette stitch)
st(s)	stitch(es)
tbl	through the back loop
tog	together
WS	wrong side
w&t	wrap and turn – take yarn to opposite side of work (between the needles), slip next stitch purlwise from LH to RH needle, return yarn to original side of work, return slipped stitch to LH needle without twisting. The stitch is now wrapped with yarn. Turn work and start next row leaving any remaining stitches unworked. When this stitch is eventually worked, knit (or purl) the wrap and the stitch together as one stitch
yo	yarnover

thank you

There are some people who deserve massive thanks – first and foremost, my Mum and Dad who are always so supportive of my chaotic creativity and who never doubt my ability to pull things off.

Mr Wool (AKA Andy Robinson) has given me an apprenticeship in business and is the most phenomenally supportive best friend that anyone could ever ask for. I could not do what I do without him.

I really could not have made this book happen without Jen Arnall-Culliford and Nic Blackmore. Jen has been gently prodding me for ages to do a pattern collection and then volunteered herself as Chief Organiser. Jen makes things happen in the most exceptionally painless and wonderful way and I am truly blessed to have her as a friend.

Nic seems to magically translate my thoughts onto paper. Despite having very clear ideas about how I want things to look, I sometimes feel I struggle to express them. It's a relief to have someone I trust to make things look awesome and, to boot, she is a complete sweetie.

Amanda France is such an accommodating and wonderful photographer. She deserves special mention too for her pioneering use of the DCR – how does anyone complete a shoot without one? The gorgeous photography in this book is all down to her.

Camilla Perkins and Lily France did a fantastic job modelling the collection with beauty and good humour.

Judy Furlong, Belinda Boaden, Elly Doyle, Lily France and Jen Arnall-Culliford are all inspiring and their input has added a nice diversity to the designs.

Kim Hobley saved us on more than one occasion with her incredibly speedy knitting – this book could not have happened without her. Frances Jago made a beautiful job of knitting the Stonor cardigan and Mel Howes deserves a medal for her marathon of endurance knitting on the Burdrop cape. Special thanks to my Auntie Pat and Auntie Yvonne for their knitting help, too.

Sarah Hatton, Mélanie Edgar and Julie Dexter provided much-appreciated pattern-checking assistance. We were grateful to Paula Hammond and Michelle Chippendale for loaning many of the clothes, props and styling accessories used on the photo-shoot.

Many thanks to The Forestry Commission and Delamere Forest for their care of our wonderful shoot location, and also to Dave France for caravan assistance and more.

And finally, Vladimir the Rat has to be given the last word – he was responsible for lots of laughter and knitting while we completed our first ever photo-shoot.

Jeni

TIBURONES

LOS GRANDES DEPREDADORES DEL OCÉANO

TIBURONES
LOS GRANDES DEPREDADORES DEL OCÉANO

John McIntyre

PaRragon

Bath · New York · Singapore · Hong Kong · Cologne · Delhi · Melbourne

Créditos de las fotografías:

© Charles Hood / Oceans Image Pictures Ltd: páginas 6, 7 (derecha), 9, 12, 13, 14 (arriba), 18-19, 20-21, 26, 34-35, 40-41, 54, 55, 61, 64-65, 77, 79, 82-83, 90, 91.

© Douglas David Seifert / Oceans Image Pictures Ltd: páginas 2-3, 16-17, 36-37, 38-39, 46-47, 48-49, 52-53, 57, 60, 62, 76, 78, 92-93, 94, 95.

© Jane Morgan / Oceans Image Pictures Ltd: página 27.
© Alex Misiewicz / Oceans Image Pictures Ltd: páginas 28-29.
© Steve Jones / Oceans Image Pictures Ltd: páginas 42, 50, 51.
© Imagestate: páginas 1, 8, 11, 14 (abajo), 15, 22, 23, 25, 32-33, 43, 45, 56, 58, 63, 81, 84-85, 86-87.
© Doug Perrine / SeaPics.com: páginas 30-31, 66-67, 74, 75 (arriba), 88-89.
© Ralph Kiefner / SeaPics.com: página 59.
© Jeff Rotman / SeaPics.com: página 75 (abajo).
© Amos Nachoum / SeaPics.com: página 80.
© Craig Bovim: página 72.
© John Crowell: página 68.
© Noah Hamilton: página 69.
© John McIntyre: página 7 (izquierda).
© Newquay Voice/Chrissie Laming: página 73 (abajo derecha).
© Chris Sullivan: página 73 (arriba izquierda, arriba derecha, abajo izquierda).
© Tony White: página 71.

ÍNDICE

INTRODUCCIÓN

La simple mención de la palabra *tiburón* desata una infinidad de emociones. Es uno de los pocos animales capaces de despertar el miedo en nuestros corazones y a la vez infundir un respeto reverencial. Los tiburones son seres legendarios, depredadores increíbles cuyos cuerpos, de líneas clásicas y aerodinámicas, han evolucionado a lo largo de más de 400 millones de años. Muchas especies casi han alcanzado la perfección física necesaria para sobrevivir en el océano.

Si preguntamos a cualquiera qué opina respecto a la mayoría de los animales de nuestro planeta, la respuesta puede ser ambivalente. Pero si preguntamos sobre los tiburones, lo más probable es que la reacción sea instantánea. Previsiblemente, las opiniones variarán de un extremo al otro. El comentario que denota mayor ignorancia, pero que lamentablemente se oye con frecuencia, es que «el tiburón bueno es el tiburón muerto».

Me llamo John McIntyre y soy periodista de la BBC y buzo veterano que ha pasado horas y horas bajo el agua, a menudo en compañía de tiburones. Mi entusiasmo y fascinación por los escualos comenzó durante la adolescencia, cuando mis padres me llevaron a ver el documental *Agua azul, muerte blanca*, innovador en su género. A lo largo de mi heterogénea carrera he informado para la BBC sobre las controvertidas inmersiones en jaula con grandes blancos, he emitido en directo desde uno de los mayores tanques de tiburones de Europa y producido la película *Sharks: The Big Ten*. Con este libro pretendo echar un vistazo a la gran variedad de tiburones que surcan nuestros mares y explicar por qué es importante comprender las razones que se ocultan tras algunos de los terroríficos accidentes relacionados con estos peligrosísimos aunque impresionantes superpredadores.

Creo que los tiburones son unos de los animales más bellos e impresionantes de la tierra. Estar en el agua con tiburones es lo más cerca que podemos llegar a estar de la naturaleza en su máxima expresión. Por eso es tan vital que hagamos todo lo posible para que el tiburón reciba la protección que merece.

Actualmente, el conocimiento sobre los tiburones ha contribuido a mejorar nuestra actitud hacia ellos; ahora sabemos que son criaturas sigilosas y dinámicas cuya ausencia causaría un grave trastorno al medio submarino. Por supuesto que hay personas que sufren mordeduras, o incluso pierden la vida, y los titulares resaltan con todo lujo de detalles estos incidentes, pero, afortunadamente, el número de estos trágicos sucesos es notablemente bajo.

Un buen amigo mío, que ha pasado años fotografiando tiburones por todo el mundo, se apropia de una conocida cita de Shakespeare para afirmar que en la reciente historia evolutiva el hombre se ha convertido en el principal enemigo del tiburón: «el tiburón es más víctima del pecado que pecador».

Se cree que existen unas 450 especies de tiburones. Su tamaño, aspecto y biología varían enormemente. Algunos tiburones ponen huevos, otros dan a luz réplicas de sus progenitores ya formadas. Incluso los hay que se convierten en caníbales dentro del útero y devoran a sus hermanos para sobrevivir.

Los dos peces más grandes del mundo son tiburones. El de mayor tamaño es el tiburón ballena gigante, seguido por el tiburón peregrino. Crecen hasta alcanzar el tamaño de un autocar y sin embargo se alimentan de los seres más diminutos del mar, el plancton. Sorprendentemente, sólo gracias a los recientes sistemas de localización vía satélite y a la tecnología informática hemos podido empezar a conocer cómo viven estos inmensos animales.

No cabe ninguna duda de cuál es el tiburón más famoso: el gran tiburón blanco. También se le conoce como jaquetón blanco y muerte blanca. Si hay algún depredador en el mundo capaz de inspirarnos el máximo respeto, ese es sin duda el gran tiburón blanco, uno de los asesinos más implacables del mar. No resulta difícil comprender por qué el hombre teme tanto a esta bestia de seis metros. ¿Es posible que pensar en un animal con dientes grandes y afilados capaz de partirnos en dos sin apenas esfuerzo nos llene instintivamente de terror?

El título que ha llegado a simbolizar ese miedo es *Tiburón*. Esta novedosa película de aventuras estremeció a los espectadores pero demonizó a los tiburones hasta el punto de provocar un número considerable de matanzas por «venganza», perpetradas por personas que se sintieron amenazadas por su mera existencia.

Sorprendentemente, muchas de las personas que han sufrido heridas terribles infligidas por tiburones defienden a sus potenciales asesinos, reconociendo que son animales increíbles que merecen nuestro respeto y protección. En algunas partes del mundo, sobre todo en Australia y Sudáfrica, se han aprobado leyes para proteger al gran tiburón blanco. En el Reino Unido se han promulgado leyes para contribuir a la salvación del tiburón peregrino, gigante, pero inofensivo.

Independientemente de su opinión personal, espero que coincida conmigo en que la historia del tiburón es realmente apasionante.

Izquierda: El autor, John McIntyre, filmando bajo el agua.

Arriba: John, cara a cara con un tiburón coralino *(Carcharhinus perezi)* en las cálidas aguas de las Bahamas.

EVOLUCIÓN

Si le piden que describa la máquina de matar perfecta, probablemente lo primero que le vendrá a la cabeza será el tiburón. El tiburón no posee ni una sola característica biológica que sea innecesaria. Cada centímetro de su cuerpo, su forma y sus órganos internos han evolucionado con un único propósito: lograr comida para poder sobrevivir. A lo largo de unos 400 millones de años, la evolución ha pulido hasta el último detalle. En la actualidad pueblan los océanos unas 450 especies de tiburón, que varían enormemente en forma y tamaño.

Un buen ejemplo es la extraña cabeza con forma de yunque del tiburón martillo. Algunos científicos creen que esta criatura es la más evolucionada de entre los tiburones. Su ancha cabeza aplanada, con los ojos situados a ambos lados, actúa como detector de metales e hidroala, y proporciona al tiburón una sensibilidad sensorial tremenda y una excelente maniobrabilidad.

Los tiburones llevan desarrollando estas características desde antes de la era de los dinosaurios. No obstante, algunas especies de tiburón han seguido inevitablemente el camino de los dinosaurios y actualmente están extintas. El más famoso de ellos es el *Carcharodon megalodon*, un auténtico gigante con unas mandíbulas tan descomunales que si aún existiera sería capaz de tragar a un hombre puesto de pie. Cada uno de sus dientes era tan grande como una mano humana. Hoy en día, los dientes fosilizados del *megalodon* se han convertido en apreciadas piezas de coleccionista.

Repasando la historia de los tiburones, los científicos han extraído mucha información de los restos fosilizados de estos peces prehistóricos, sobre todo de sus dientes, que suelen estar perfectamente conservados. Es frecuente que los dientes sean lo único que permanezca fosilizado, porque los tiburones carecen de esqueleto óseo. En vez de ello, su estructura está formada por un material resistente y flexible llamado cartílago, por lo que han sido asignados al grupo científico de los elasmobranquios, que incluye a las rayas y algunos de los peces menos conocidos que habitan en las profundidades marinas. Estar dotado de un esqueleto cartilaginoso equivaldría en un coche deportivo a tener un chasis de fibra de carbono ligera pero fuerte. En el caso del tiburón, el diseño es realmente producto de las fuerzas revolucionarias de la naturaleza. Otra diferencia

crucial entre los tiburones y los peces osteictios reside en que los tiburones carecen de vejiga natatoria. La vejiga natatoria de un pez actúa como el chaleco hidrostático de un buceador. A medida que éste se sumerge y aumenta la presión del agua, el buzo sólo tiene que bombear más aire dentro del chaleco para mantener una flotabilidad neutra y permanecer así a la profundidad deseada.

El tiburón, sin embargo, depende de su enorme hígado, que contiene un fino aceite que es más ligero que el agua y le ayuda a flotar. Incluso con este gran hígado, el tiburón sigue siendo más pesado que el agua y tiene tendencia a hundirse. Por este motivo, con algunas excepciones, los tiburones tienen que nadar constantemente durante toda su vida. Como pájaros flotando en el viento, los tiburones son los señores de las corrientes oceánicas. Se deslizan por las aguas con el mínimo esfuerzo, guardando una energía ganada a pulso para los arranques de velocidad indispensables durante una cacería.

A pesar del pequeño tamaño de su cerebro, las credenciales evolutivas del tiburón como el asesino número uno de los mares parecen sacadas de las especificaciones de un mortífero ingenio militar del futuro. Tal vez el arma más extraordinaria de los escualos sean los desarrollados órganos sensoriales que aparecen como pequeños puntos sobre el morro. Se trata en realidad de diminutas cavidades rellenas de una sustancia gelatinosa capaz de detectar corrientes eléctricas ínfimas. Estos electrorreceptores son conocidos como ampollas de Lorenzini. Cuando un pez lucha o está muriéndose, sus músculos emiten señales eléctricas apenas perceptibles. Incluso a distancia, el tiburón es capaz de detectarlas. Observando este comportamiento en las Bahamas, me asombraron tanto las distancias recorridas como la frenética velocidad a la que los

Páginas anteriores

Página 8: El feroz aspecto de la dentadura del tiburón toro *(Carcharias taurus)* le confiere una apariencia temible que contradice su carácter, generalmente dócil.

Página 9: Un tiburón martillo gigante *(Sphyrna mokarran)* patrullando por las Bahamas cerca de la superficie y ofreciendo una excelente perspectiva de su cabeza con forma de hidroala.

Diente fosilizado de cinco millones de años de antigüedad; perteneció al tiburón más grande jamás conocido, el *Carcharodon megalodon.*

tiburones coralinos reaccionaban ante los pequeños peces heridos tendidos sobre un arrecife.

Por tanto, es comprensible que la empresa de desarrollar un sistema fiable de protección frente a los tiburones empezara a dar resultados cuando se utilizó la electricidad como medio de defensa. Generando campos eléctricos relativamente fuertes alrededor de un buceador, los científicos descubrieron que podían bloquear de forma eficaz los sentidos del tiburón y hacer que hasta el más grande de ellos diera media vuelta.

También hay una fina línea que discurre a lo largo de todo el cuerpo del tiburón. Se conoce como línea lateral y permite al tiburón detectar vibraciones mínimas en el agua que lo rodea y sentir así la presencia de otros animales. El sofisticado despliegue de sentidos del tiburón le permite detectar hasta el más minúsculo campo magnético en el mar, lo que le ayuda a navegar con precisión.

El tiburón posee una vista excelente, una fantástica sensibilidad auditiva y, por supuesto, un olfato perfecto. Un ejemplo asombroso de sus habilidades olfativas es su capacidad de detectar una gota de sangre entre un millón de gotas de agua. La piel presenta también un diseño ingenioso, ya que está cubierta por miles de hileras de minúsculos dientes modificados, llamados dentículos dérmicos. Si uno acaricia a un tiburón desde el morro hacia la cola, la piel tiene un tacto sedoso. Si lo hace en la dirección contraria, es probable que acabe con su propia piel hecha jirones. Esta increíble característica de diseño no sólo proporciona al tiburón una recia protección externa, también dota al animal de un excelente hidrodinamismo.

Dado que los tiburones son superpredadores en todas las áreas de los océanos, han tenido que adaptarse a sus entornos locales. El tiburón ángel, por ejemplo, acecha en la arena del fondo oceánico como una trampa silenciosa, esperando para engullir a las desprevenidas presas que nadan por los alrededores. Los tiburones sierra están dotados de singulares hocicos serrados, parecidos a armas medievales. La lista incluye tiburones duende, tiburones cocodrilo, tiburones gato, tiburones zorro… El diseño de cada uno de ellos se ha ido transformando con la evolución a lo largo de millones de años para garantizar la supervivencia en las circunstancias más extremas, ya sea en las llanuras abisales de las profundidades, las aguas rocosas poco profundas, los arrecifes de coral o el mar abierto. Los tiburones merodean por los rincones más insospechados del planeta, desde las aguas heladas del Ártico hasta los cálidos arrecifes caribeños.

Algunos tiburones paren crías, mientras que otros desovan. Y no todos los tiburones son peligrosos para el hombre, pues los de mayor tamaño son totalmente inofensivos. Tanto el tiburón ballena gigante como su primo, el tiburón peregrino, viven de las presas más minúsculas: plancton y peces pequeños.

Los tiburones son, sin duda, una obra maestra de la evolución. Si programásemos hoy en día una computadora para que diseñase la máquina de matar submarina perfecta, no sería de extrañar que el resultado se pareciese notablemente a un tiburón.

El tiburón toro *(Carcharias taurus)* fue la primera especie en recibir protección legal en Australia en 1984.

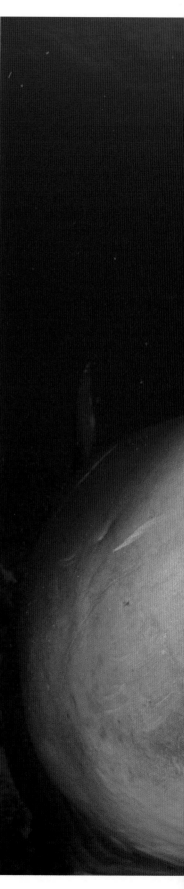

Arriba: El tiburón cornudo *(Heterodontus francisci)* alcanza sólo 1 m de longitud y está perfectamente adaptado para cazar en las zonas rocosas del Pacífico. Esto demuestra lo bien que cada especie de tiburón ha evolucionado para adaptarse a su propio entorno.

Derecha: El marrajo dientuso *(Isurus oxyrinchus)* es uno de los tiburones más veloces del océano, capaz de cazar a los ágiles atunes y a las agujas. Este ejemplar fue fotografiado en el Mar Rojo.

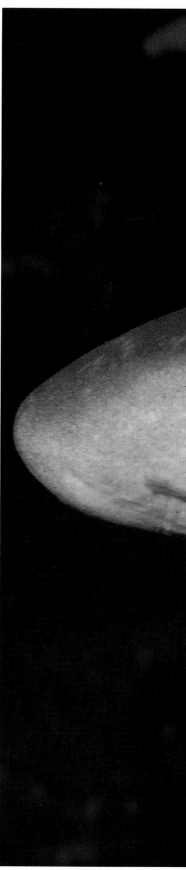

Arriba: Los tiburones punti-blancos *(Triaenodon obesus)* son comunes en los océanos tropicales. Son prácticamente inofensivos para los humanos, aunque sean incansables caza-dores nocturnos que persiguen en grupo a los peces.

Derecha: Los tiburones azu-les *(Prionace glauca)* viven en mar abierto y pueden crecer hasta unos 3,5 m de longitud. Son uno de los tiburones más elegantes.

Página siguiente: Los tibu-rones toro *(Carcharias taurus)* son los preferidos de los acua-rios, porque son relativamente fáciles de cuidar y sus dientes resultan impresionantes.

Los tiburones martillo *(Sphyrna lewini)* suelen formar grandes cardúmenes alrededor de montículos marinos naturales en lugares como la Isla del Coco, en las costas de Costa Rica. Forman cola en estas áreas para que los peces mariposa los desparasiten.

El tiburón martillo gigante
(Sphyrna mokarran) es una
de las especies más raras
de ver o fotografiar. Puede
alcanzar una longitud de unos
6 m y pesar hasta 450 kg.
Su dieta incluye tiburones de
menor tamaño y rayas.

Esta asombrosa imagen de un tiburón martillo gigante fue tomada frontalmente por el fotógrafo submarino Charles Hood en las Bahamas. Casi parece un avión de combate de alta tecnología, con sus ojos escudriñadores, que presentan una separación de 1,5 m entre sí. Uno de los manjares favoritos del tiburón martillo gigante es la raya venenosa. Usa su ancha cabeza para acorralar la raya contra el lecho marino y luego la inmoviliza mordiendo un trozo de su aleta pectoral.

TIBURONES CLÁSICOS

Las líneas clásicas y elegantes de algunos tiburones los han convertido en los auténticos «supermodelos» del mar. Del mismo modo que una bella modelo puede aumentar las ventas de una revista, las publicaciones de buceo e historia natural se han percatado de que sus ventas se disparan cuando un tiburón ocupa su portada. Uno de los más fotografiados es el tiburón coralino, el más fácil de identificar. Este grupo abarca desde los pendencieros tiburones coralinos del Caribe hasta el tiburón gris. Estas dos especies y algunos de sus parientes, de aspecto similar, se encuentran en abundancia en los mares tropicales. Naturalmente, su aspecto presenta un gran número de sutiles variaciones en función de la zona del mundo en la que se encuentren.

A título orientativo, la apariencia clásica de un tiburón es un cuerpo alargado con forma de torpedo de color grisáceo o amarronado con el vientre blanco. La forma más habitual consta de cinco aberturas branquiales y ocho aletas, la más conocida de las cuales es la primera dorsal, la que suele sobresalir del agua y «matar de miedo» a los asustados bañistas. Las aletas situadas junto a las aberturas branquiales son conocidas como pectorales, y la

aleta de la cola recibe el nombre científico de aleta caudal. El conjunto se completa con otras cuatro aletas de menor tamaño. Los tiburones macho poseen dos cláspers, que son extensiones de las aletas pélvicas; son los órganos sexuales aunque, por si se lo ha preguntado, no usa los dos a la vez.

Las especies clásicas pertenecen a la familia de los tiburones réquiem *(Carcharhinidae)* que agrupa a más de la mitad de las poblaciones de tiburones conocidas. Como consecuencia de su amplia presencia, estadísticamente son los tiburones responsables de la mayoría de muertes y heridas causadas por ataques de tiburón. El tiburón «clásico» más famoso de todos, el gran blanco, no pertenece a este grupo, sino que es un tiburón lámnido *(Lamnidae)*, por lo que este depredador en mayúsculas es objeto de un capítulo propio (véase la página 76).

La familia de los tiburones réquiem incluye especies conocidas por cualquier espectador de documentales de naturaleza, como el poderoso tiburón sarda, el esbelto tiburón azul y el peso pesado y «basurero del océano», el tiburón tigre.

Como la mayoría de los miembros de la comunidad de superpredadores del océano, los tiburones

réquiem desempeñan un papel fundamental en la conservación del equilibrio medioambiental. Su función es cazar presas enfermas, heridas o débiles, lo que demuestra una vez más la naturaleza despiadada del principio de la supervivencia del más apto.

Algunos de estos tiburones, sobre todo los tiburones puntiblancos, de menor tamaño, cazan en manada, como los perros salvajes. Durante la noche patrullan por los arrecifes atentos al menor movimiento de sus presas. Uno de los mejores lugares del mundo para observar este comportamiento es la lejana Isla del Coco, en el Pacífico. Aquí se reúnen los puntiblancos a centenares, merodeando por el rocoso fondo marino como bandas de delincuentes juveniles pavoneándose por las calles. Cuando avistan un pez, los tiburones bombardean el arrecife. Su piel es tan dura que pueden meter la cabeza en los rincones y ranuras más pequeños sin resultar dañados. Después de una noche de actividad frenética, pasan el día o bien descansando sobre el lecho marino o surcando las termoclinas que rodean la isla. Los puntiblancos son de los pocos tiburones capaces de bombear agua por sus agallas para poder respirar mientras permanecen quietos.

Los puntiblancos y el tiburón gris, de líneas más clásicas, son observados con frecuencia por los buceadores. Los primeros son extremadamente dóciles, pero los tiburones grises pueden ser agresivos si se les provoca. Crecen hasta superar los 2 m de longitud. Se pasan los días en movimiento y también son cazadores nocturnos. Cuando un tiburón gris se siente amenazado de cualquier forma, adopta una postura sumamente ofensiva. Primero, el tiburón baja sus aletas pectorales. Si un buceador, u otro tiburón, no capta el mensaje, el animal pasa al siguiente nivel, esto es, arquear la espalda. Es momento de retirarse. El tiburón puede atacar a gran velocidad y las heridas resultantes pueden ser muy graves.

Páginas anteriores

Página 22: Tiburón coralino con una rémora en el vientre.

Página 23: El tiburón de puntas negras *(Carcharhinus melanopterus)* es el habitante habitual de las lagunas y los arrecifes de los océanos Pacífico e Índico. Éstos fueron vistos en las aguas de Tahití.

Subiendo en la jerarquía de los tiburones réquiem nos encontramos con uno de los escualos más peligrosos del mundo, el musculoso tiburón sarda, de hasta 3,5 m de longitud. Son los asesinos más frecuentes de seres humanos, más incluso que los tiburones blancos. Una de las razones es que poseen la rara habilidad de poder moverse tanto en agua dulce como en agua salada. Se han descubierto tiburones sarda en ríos de aguas turbias, varios kilómetros tierra adentro. En aquellos lugares donde la gente depende del río para su sustento, como Sudáfrica y Suramérica, el riesgo de ser atacado por un tiburón es considerable. Muchos de estos incidentes no quedan registrados debido al remoto emplazamiento de estas aldeas.

En lo alto de la pirámide se encuentra el impresionante tiburón tigre. Estos tiburones son conocidos por devorar absolutamente cualquier cosa que se ponga en su camino. Se han encontrado las cosas más extrañas en los estómagos de especímenes muertos, como matrículas de coches, la tibia de un niño, cornamentas, perros, latas e incluso llantas.

Algunos de los tiburones tigre más grandes registrados han llegado a superar los 5 o 6 m. Como su nombre sugiere, se identifican fácilmente por sus marcas atigradas. En principio, estos predadores parecen cautelosos y tímidos, pero cuidado: este tiburón jamás debe subestimarse.

Mientras que los tiburones tigres tienden a verse en parejas o en tríos otros miembros de la familia réquiem prefieren la fuerza del grupo. Asimismo, en las aguas repletas de alimentos alrededor de la Isla del Coco se puede ver al fotogénico tiburón jaquetón formando enormes cardúmenes. Este tipo de tiburón se conoce como «oceánico» o «pelágico», lo que significa que pasa la mayor parte de su vida en mar abierto.

A la hora de reproducirse, los tiburones réquiem comparten características con los mamíferos. No sólo fertilizan sus huevos internamente, sino que paren pequeños tiburones totalmente formados. Durante la reproducción, el tiburón macho muerde a la hembra y la retiene así durante el apareamiento, lo que acostumbra a dejar en ellas unas cicatrices, a veces llamadas «mordiscos de amor».

Un tiburón gris puede parir entre una y seis crías después de un largo periodo de gestación que dura aproximadamente un año. Éste sería el único punto débil en el dominio de los tiburones sobre los océanos del planeta. Un tiburón puede tardar hasta siete años en alcanzar la madurez sexual. En las zonas donde la población de tiburones se ha visto reducida drásticamente debido a la sobrepesca es difícil, y en algunos casos imposible, conservar dichas poblaciones. Resulta complicado obtener datos científicos exactos sobre el número de tiburones, pero hay muchas organizaciones conservacionistas, además del Programa de las Naciones Unidas para el Medio Ambiente, que están convencidas de que, a menos que esta industria se reduzca de forma masiva, los tiburones clásicos tienen los días contados.

El tiburón jaquetón *(Carcharhinus falciformis)* es un tiburón oceánico grande y esbelto que alcanza una longitud de unos 3,5 m. Acostumbran a nadar formando grandes cardúmenes en aguas profundas, donde cazan peces y calamares.

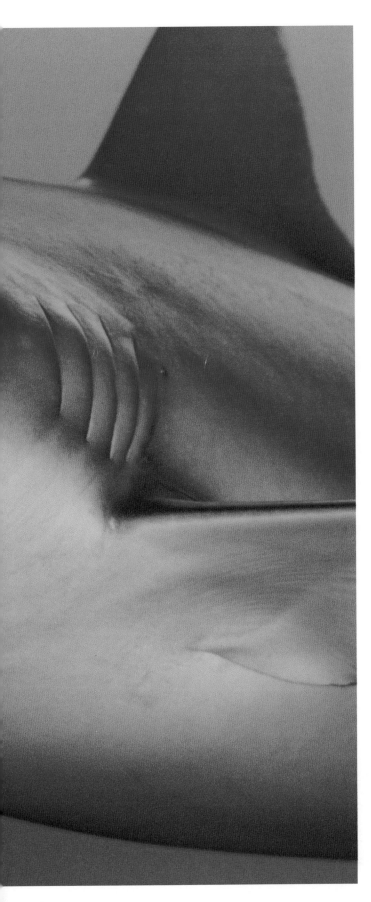

Izquierda: Los tiburones grises *(Carcharhinus amblyrhynchos)* pueden tener mal genio si se les provoca. Suelen verse en las fuertes corrientes que se producen en lugares como el Mar Rojo, las Maldivas y Australia.

Arriba: Este impresionante puntiblanco oceánico *(Carcharhinus longimanus)* fue fotografiado en el Mar Rojo egipcio acompañado por el omnipresente pez piloto; se cree que estos últimos se alimentan de las sobras de la comida del tiburón. En las zonas en las que comparten el mismo hábitat, los puntiblancos oceánicos se suelen encontrar nadando con grandes grupos de ballenas piloto, y las siguen incluso a aguas profundas.

Los tiburones de puntas negras
(Carcharhinus melanopterus)
suelen usar bancos de barra-
cudas como tapadera, tal y
como se muestra aquí en Ras
Mohamed, en el Mar Rojo,
donde suelen verse a menudo
durante los meses estivales.

El tiburón tigre *(Galeocerdo cuvier)* alcanza los 5,5 m de longitud y tiene fama de ser el basurero de los océanos, ya que se come prácticamente todo lo que pueda tragar mientras busca comida. Están considerados potencialmente peligrosos para bañistas y submarinistas.

Estos pequeños peces están «haciendo autoestop» en la onda de presión creada por un tiburón gris en las Bahamas, una forma excelente de viajar gratis y aprovechar restos de comida que sobran cuando el anfitrión ha terminado de alimentarse.

Los tiburones coralinos
(Carcharhinus perezi) son
probablemente los tiburones
más fotografiados, ya que
no suelen alterarse por la
presencia de submarinistas.
Son de un color entre gris y
marrón grisáceo, tienen el
vientre blanco y alcanzan
una longitud de unos 3 m.

Los comederos para tiburones
son un gran negocio. Se calcula que cada ejemplar vivo tiene
un valor de unos 84.000 euros
(100.000 dólares) anuales
para las economías locales
gracias al turismo generado
por la gente que quiere nadar
con tiburones. En las Maldivas,
por ejemplo, los buceadores
gastan aproximadamente
1,9 millones de euros (2,3 millones de dólares) anuales en
inmersiones con tiburones.
Se estima que esto multiplica
por cien los beneficios por
exportación de carne de escua-
lo. Esta fotografía de tiburones
alimentándose fue tomada en
Walker's Cay, en las Bahamas.

Los tiburones sarda *(Carcharhinus leucas)* son probablemente los más peligrosos de los mares, ya que son responsables de más muertes humanas que ningún otro tiburón. Son seres poderosos pero en Walker's Cay, en las Bahamas, la gente bucea con ellos a 2 m de profundidad. Estos nadadores están a salvo, porque el agua es límpida y los tiburones solamente se interesan por los peces. Sus sentidos son tan agudos que pueden distinguir con facilidad entre las personas y su comida favorita. Sin embargo, hay que evitarlos a toda costa en aguas turbias.

Los tiburones coralinos
suelen acercarse a centímetros de la cámara o de las
gafas del submarinista antes
de dar la vuelta en el último
segundo. Estos tiburones no
suelen considerarse agresivos
para los buzos, pero se han
registrado casos de ataques
a personas.

GIGANTES DEL OCÉANO

No todos los tiburones son peligrosos. De hecho, los dos escualos más grandes, y por tanto los dos peces de mayor tamaño que surcan los océanos, se alimentan de algo tan poco espectacular como el diminuto plancton. Ambos han sido bautizados como los gigantes gentiles del océano. El más grande es el elegante tiburón ballena, llamado así por su inmenso tamaño. El segundo en el *ranking* es el tiburón peregrino, no tan elegante y de aspecto ligeramente más prehistórico, que habita en aguas más frías. Los principales programas de investigación sobre estos peces se centran actualmente en los bancos de tiburones peregrinos que patrullan por las costas británicas.

En el caso del tiburón ballena, que muestra un perfil distintivo, las imponentes imágenes de buceadores afanándose por seguir el ritmo de estas gigantescas criaturas dan una idea de su tamaño. Se sabe que alcanzan unos 12 m de largo, aunque hay informes de tiburones ballena descomunales de hasta 18 m, mayores que algunas de las grandes ballenas, que son, como es sabido, mamíferos. Aunque es difícil calcular el peso medio del pez más grande del mundo, se han registrado especímenes de más de 8.000 kg, con hígados enormes de casi una tonelada.

Sin embargo, para ser animales tan grandes, sus ojos son relativamente pequeños. Al igual que en el caso del tiburón peregrino, parece que la mayor virtud de estos enormes escualos reside en sus inmensas bocas. En ese sentido, son muy parecidos a las ballenas. Cuando nadan cerca de la superficie en busca de su humilde dieta, su eficiente sistema de alimentación por filtrado tamiza el alimento entre los miles de litros de agua que traga cada hora. Un cineasta submarino que se enfrentó a su primer tiburón peregrino en las costas de Cornualles casi no daba crédito a lo que veía: «Cuando vi esa boca gigante que se me acercaba, realmente pensé que me iba a tragar entero». Afortunadamente, el peligro era mínimo. Ni el tiburón ballena ni el peregrino son capaces de tragar comida de mayor tamaño que el pescado que se sirve en un restaurante.

Ambos tiburones recorren miles de kilómetros al año en busca de su alimento principal. Los sistemas actuales de seguimiento vía satélite se usan cada vez más para seguir sus movimientos con fines científicos. Curiosamente, el tiburón ballena es uno

de los animales más difíciles de encontrar, pese a su enorme tamaño. En el Mar Rojo, donde el equipo pionero de buceadores formado por el matrimonio Hans y Lotte Hass grabó por primera vez un tiburón ballena en 1949, los avistamientos son bastante escasos hoy en día. Las personas que han trabajado como guías de inmersión durante diez años o más suelen afirmar que no han visto más de uno o dos en toda su carrera. Sin embargo, hay lugares donde aumentan las posibilidades de encontrar a este dinosaurio de las profundidades. En un diminuto rincón del mundo conocido como Ningaloo Reef, en el noroeste australiano, se ha desarrollado una pequeña industria alrededor de los avistamientos, prácticamente garantizados, del *Rhincodon typus*, su nombre científico. Para el pequeño grupo de científicos, turistas y submarinistas que se reúnen allí todos los años en febrero y marzo, Ningaloo es mágico. Es también el arrecife donde este autor se encontró con su primer tiburón ballena.

La combinación del clima y las corrientes favorables parecen crear las condiciones perfectas para satisfacer el inagotable apetito del tiburón ballena. Eso se debe a que también es el momento en el que los arrecifes de coral desovan, lo que convierte los mares circundantes en un auténtico festín de microorganismos. Incluso así, los buceadores necesitan ayuda para encontrar a los peces más grandes del océano. Para garantizar una alta tasa de éxito, los turoperadores que organizan estas actividades usan pequeños aeroplanos o ultraligeros a la caza de reveladoras sombras gigantes errando por el agua. El piloto informa de la posición exacta del animal y los turistas se sumergen en el agua en el camino del tiburón ballena, a veces bastante cerca de los tiburones tigre, mucho más mortíferos, que también van a Ningaloo para aprovechar la abundancia de alimento. Después, durante unos breves pero excitantes minutos, el nadador bracea junto al enorme tiburón

Páginas anteriores

Página 42: Un tiburón ballena *(Rhincodon typus)* atrae a varios compañeros de viaje, como grandes rémoras y bancos de fusileros.
Página 43: Este buceador con tubo parece enano junto al mayor tiburón del mundo, pero no tema, es completamente inofensivo.

ballena, ante cuya presencia no puede más que sentirse diminuto. Es una experiencia increíble. Sin embargo, más de un buceador con tubo respirador ha estado a punto de pasarlo muy mal en alguna ocasión, al buscar emociones fuertes cabalgando agarrado a las aletas del tiburón. Cuando los submarinistas demasiado ambiciosos asustan a los tiburones ballena, éstos suelen huir a las profundidades. Para algunos individuos es una experiencia terrorífica, ya que se dan cuenta de repente de que se están sumergiendo en aguas peligrosamente profundas y se adueña de ellos la desesperación por coger aire. Muchos operadores ven ahora con ojo crítico a los buceadores que cabalgan encima de los tiburones, ya que temen que pueda tener un efecto adverso en el comportamiento del animal. Actualmente, en el oeste de Australia, cabalgar sobre un tiburón ballena se considera un delito.

En las aguas británicas las leyes también protegen al primo, ligeramente más pequeño, del tiburón ballena, el tiburón peregrino. Durante los meses estivales estos torpones rumiantes marinos efectúan su aparición anual en las costas de Cornualles, la isla de Man y el oeste de Escocia, haciendo las delicias de veraneantes y científicos. Hubo una época en que sus enormes aletas los convirtieron en uno de los objetivos del lucrativo mercado de la sopa de aleta de tiburón. También fueron cazados sin piedad debido a sus grandes hígados, que contienen un aceite de gran calidad usado como combustible para lámparas, entre otras cosas. Las poblaciones de tiburones peregrinos descendieron considerablemente, pero por suerte estas prácticas pertenecen al pasado, al menos en el Reino Unido.

Sin embargo, en los mares verdes y relativamente fríos de las islas británicas a la gente le ha costado muchos años acostumbrarse a ver una aleta de tiburón gris oscuro de 2 m de altura asomando por la superficie no muy lejos de la orilla. De hecho, más de una vez algún guardacostas ha dado la alarma para sacar a la gente del agua, ante el temor de que se repitiese una escena de *Tiburón* durante su turno. Al igual que el tiburón ballena, al peregrino sólo le interesa el diminuto plancton y las larvas de crustáceos que amarillean las aguas durante el verano.

Ellos también se han convertido en una atracción turística, con barcos buscando cardúmenes de hasta 30 o 40 animales que pescan lentamente, pero con determinación, por los canales de Inglaterra e Irlanda en busca de su sustento. Un tiburón peregrino de buen tamaño alcanza una longitud de unos 10 m y tiene una esperanza de vida de hasta 50 años. Incluso al nacer (estos tiburones paren crías vivas) ya tienen un tamaño descomunal, de más de 1 m, y están listos para lanzarse al mundo. Aunque un espécimen adulto podría causar daños graves a los humanos, hay constancia de que han pasado junto a adultos y niños, rozándolos suavemente, sin producirles ni un rasguño.

El seguimiento por satélite y los estudios fotográficos han demostrado que los tiburones peregrinos que se avistan año tras año en las aguas del Reino Unido son en realidad residentes permanentes. Puede que cubran grandes distancias alrededor de la costa y que en invierno se sumerjan en aguas más profundas, pero permanecen en el mismo territorio. Esta información crucial ha servido para proteger a los tiburones. El hecho de saber que son residentes significa que las leyes que los protegen son mucho más efectivas que si los animales fueran simples visitantes migratorios.

Puede que no sea tan glamouroso como el ballena, pero incluso así el tiburón peregrino se ha ganado un amplio club de fans. Así que si visita las islas británicas y avista una gran aleta dorsal cerca de la orilla puede considerarse afortunado. Lejos de encontrarse ante un terrorífico devorador de hombres, estará ante un inofensivo habitante de la zona que resulta ser un tiburón enorme.

Los tiburones ballena pueden alcanzar unos 18 m de longitud. Viajan miles de kilómetros cada año en busca de plancton, peces pequeños y calamares, que consumen en cantidades enormes.

En determinados momentos del año los tiburones ballena se reúnen en las costas de lugares como Ningaloo, en el oeste de Australia, las Seychelles y Honduras para alimentarse de las abundantes floraciones de zooplancton y aprovechar el desove anual de los corales.

A pesar de ser el mayor
pez del océano, es poco
frecuente avistar un tiburón
ballena. Los programas de
seguimiento por satélite han
empezado recientemente a
arrojar pistas sobre sus patrones de comportamiento.

Arriba: Un tiburón ballena nada en las aguas ricas en nutrientes rodeado por un denso banco de fusileros. La presencia de estos animales indica la existencia de una fuente de alimento abundante.

Derecha: Los tiburones ballena reciben protección oficial en varios países, entre ellos Australia, Honduras, India, Filipinas y Estados Unidos. Sin embargo, siguen siendo cazados legal e ilegalmente en algunas partes de Asia.

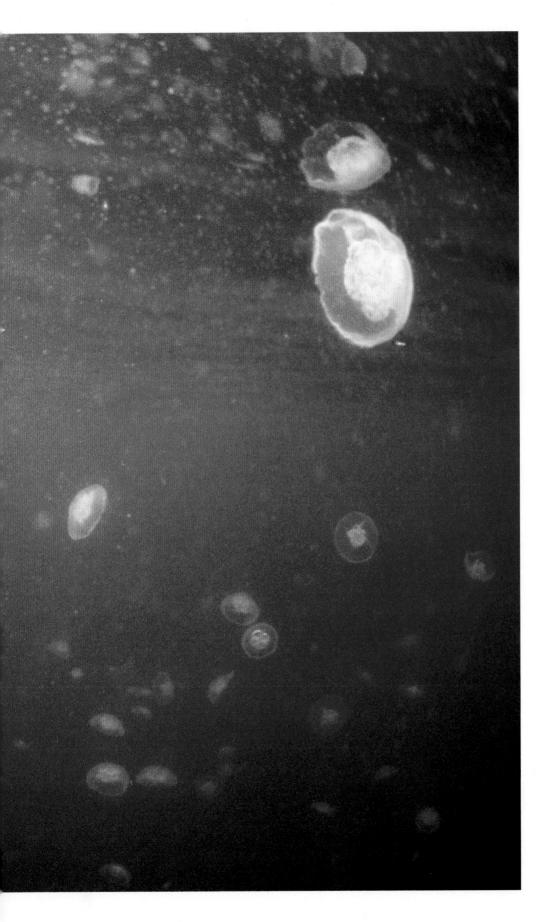

Un tiburón peregrino
(Cetorhinus maximus) con
la boca abierta para filtrar
plancton entre las medusas,
cerca de la isla de Man. Estos
tiburones gigantes se congre-
gan a veces por centenares
durante los meses de verano
y pueden avistarse fácilmente
desde la costa cuando el mar
está en calma.

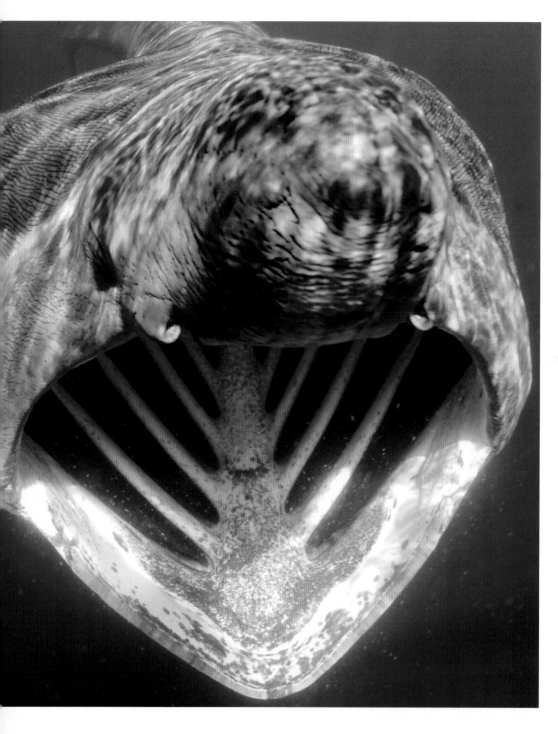

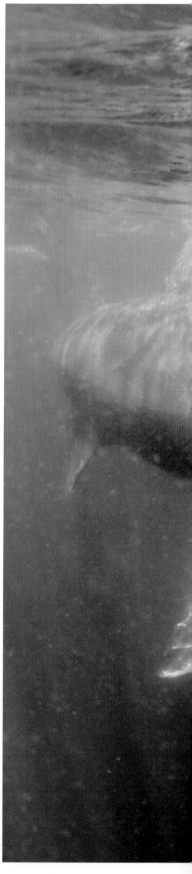

Los tiburones peregrinos se alimentan nadando con sus enormes bocas totalmente abiertas, filtrando plancton y animales microscópicos del agua mediante sus branquispinas (unos pequeños dispositivos de filtrado parecidos a cerdas situados sobre las agallas). Las branquispinas del tiburón peregrino pueden procesar hasta 2.000 toneladas de agua por hora. De vez en cuando, el tiburón cierra las agallas y «reenvía» la comida a la garganta, donde la ingiere.

TIBURONES Y HUMANOS

Estar cara a cara con un tiburón es una de las emociones que a mucha gente le gustaría experimentar antes de morir. Curiosamente, cuatro de las cinco actividades más emocionantes están relacionadas con las maravillas del gran azul. Si nadar con delfines es el sueño número uno, bucear con tiburones ocupa un meritorio quinto puesto.

Para la gente que siente un miedo innato hacia los tiburones, el desafío puede ser extremadamente difícil, incluso aterrador, pero hoy en día organizarlo es tan fácil como reservar un viaje por Internet.

La actitud hacia los tiburones ha cambiado considerablemente en las últimas décadas. No hace tanto, mucha gente creía que «el tiburón bueno era el tiburón muerto». Los pioneros del cine submarino eran de las pocas personas lo bastante valientes como para entrar en el agua con tiburones, ya que era muy poco lo que se sabía sobre estos asesinos potenciales. Han pasado décadas desde que gente como Jacques Cousteau, Hans y Lotte Hass, Stan Waterman y la pareja australiana Ron y Valerie Taylor llevaran imágenes fascinantes del mundo marino a nuestra sala de estar. Los fotogramas de personas nadando con tiburones bastaban para

acelerar el pulso a los telespectadores, más aún si cabe a los submarinistas más inseguros y aprensivos.

La famosa película *Agua azul, muerte blanca* (1971) fue el primer gran documental sobre los tiburones blancos. El viaje épico de Peter Gimbel llevó al equipo alrededor de medio mundo, pero las imágenes de los Taylor y otros buceadores abandonando la seguridad de sus jaulas para entrar en el agua mientras los tiburones puntiblancos devoraban el cadáver de un cachalote eran impactantes. El cadáver de una ballena no bastó para atraer a los grandes blancos, pero al final el equipo consiguió localizar al depredador número uno y el filme resultante fue alabado por muchos como la película de tiburones más impactante de su época.

No es de extrañar que Hollywood no pudiera resistirse a la tentación de incluir tiburones en sus producciones. En las Bahamas, los productores de las películas de James Bond contrataron a buceadores locales para que trabajaran con tiburones coralinos y tigre en la creación de escenarios mortales para su héroe. Las películas *Nunca digas nunca jamás* y *Sólo para tus ojos* convirtieron la isla de Nassau en uno de los primeros grandes destinos de buceo con

No intente esto en casa, ni siquiera con un traje de malla metálica, pues un tiburón azul *(Prionace glauca)* decidido puede resultar de lo más agresivo cuando hay comida de por medio.

tiburones. La gente pagaba grandes cantidades de dinero para estar a unos pocos centímetros de aquellas famosas criaturas.

Sin embargo, para que las empresas de buceo pudieran aumentar su negocio necesitaban incentivar a ambas partes; los tiburones necesitaban una razón para montar un espectáculo. Sólo había una forma: los buceadores se convirtieron en *«cowboys* de tiburones» armados con cubos de pescado. Los escualos no tardaron en darse cuenta de que iban a sacar tajada y respondieron ansiosamente. Con docenas de tiburones coralinos viniendo a por su cena (con una falta absoluta de modales) los submarinistas que llevaban la comida necesitaban protección. Valerie Taylor y otros probaron con éxito los trajes de malla metálica que son ahora habituales en todos los comederos de tiburones.

Páginas anteriores

Página 56: Un encuentro cara a cara con un tiburón es siempre una experiencia memorable para cualquier submarinista.

Página 57: Turismo con tiburones en acción: decenas de tiburones coralinos *(Carcharhinus perezi)* aparecen para comer gratis en las Bahamas, lo que brinda a los invitados de pago una de las experiencias más emocionantes que ofrece la naturaleza.

Hay comederos en muchos lugares del trópico. Por el precio de una cena modesta para dos es posible ver como los tiburones se zampan un menú de atunes y jureles. El buceador, a menudo protegido por un traje de malla o al menos guantes de malla de acero y protecciones en los brazos, suele bajar la carnada al lecho marino en una caja sellada. A continuación se pide a los submarinistas invitados que formen un semicírculo a unos 5 o 6 m del alimentador. A los pocos minutos los tiburones coralinos efectúan su bulliciosa aparición. A los buceadores inexpertos les falta el aliento, sobre todo cuando algunos de los animales nadan literalmente entre sus piernas. Los tiburones no tardan en empezar a tomar el pescado directamente de la mano del buzo o de la punta de una barra de acero. En este punto la cosa se descontrola. Los tiburones llegan incluso a chocar con los submarinistas mientras compiten por el pescado gratuito. Se han producido situaciones en las que han mordido a buceadores por accidente (a veces provocándoles heridas graves) pero teniendo en cuenta las miles de inmersiones que se producen cada año, desde un punto de vista estadístico, no es más peligroso que, por ejemplo, montar en bicicleta.

Hay diversas razones por las que la gente quiere meterse en el agua con tiburones. Algunos disfrutan de la inyección de adrenalina, otros intentan superar una fobia y otros creen que el tiburón es una criatura potencialmente peligrosa aunque bella que debe ser antes admirada que temida. Muchas personas cambian su actitud hacia los tiburones después de tener contacto con ellos. La palabra que usa la mayoría tras la inmersión es *respeto*.

La industria del tiburón es un gran negocio. Al igual que los avistamientos de ballenas, ha ayudado a convencer a la gente de que los escualos valen más vivos que muertos. Se calcula que un tiburón vivo puede generar para una economía local, gracias al ecoturismo, un beneficio de 84.000 euros (100.000 dólares).

Aunque Jacques Cousteau nos introdujese a muchos de nosotros en la magia de silencioso mundo submarino, la obsesión moderna por la notoriedad se ha traducido en miles de horas de programas televisivos sobre los tiburones a cargo de científicos entusiastas o presentadores famosos.

Las cadenas dedican semanas enteras exclusivamente a los tiburones, intentando llevar al límite la ciencia y la interacción humana. En Dangerous Reef, en el sur de Australia, y en la isla de Dyer, en Sudáfrica, la controvertida moda del buceo en jaula con grandes blancos se ha puesto al alcance de cualquier turista. Los que buscan emociones fuertes pueden disfrutar de un sobrecogedor encuentro desde la seguridad de una sólida jaula de acero.

Sin embargo, expertos en tiburones como Andre Hartman fueron los primeros en poner su corazón a mil por hora acariciando a grandes blancos en el morro cuando asomaban la cabeza fuera del agua para inspeccionar los barcos. Hartman y otros pusieron a prueba sus nervios hasta límites insospechados al atreverse con el buceo libre con grandes blancos sin más protección que su ingenio. Dado que los tiburones pueden detectar fácilmente la aceleración del ritmo cardíaco, esta experiencia no es apta para gente nerviosa, pero para cualquier persona que sea lo suficientemente valiente como para enfrentarse cara a cara con el depredador más famoso de la tierra, ésta debe de ser sin duda una de las experiencias más extremas en la naturaleza.

¡No apto para miedosos o aficionados! El buceador Michael Rutzen toca el hocico de un gran tiburón blanco *(Carcharodon carcharias)* en Sudáfrica.

Arriba: El premiado fotógrafo submarino Douglas David Seifert sacó esas fotos durante una expedición en busca de tiburones blancos en las costas de la isla de Guadalupe, en México. Ese es uno de los principales destinos actualmente para ver al tiburón número uno en aguas azules y cristalinas. La carnada hecha con carne de atún, sangre de pescado y aceite se usa para atraer a los tiburones cerca de las jaulas.

Derecha: Un submarinista observa los tiburones desde la relativa seguridad de una jaula de acero. Este tipo de ecoturismo se empezó a desarrollar en el sur de Australia y Sudáfrica, lugares con grandes poblaciones de tiburones blancos.

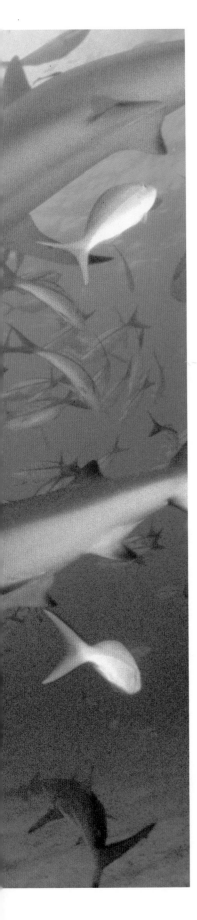

Izquierda: La alimentación de tiburones en las Bahamas se convirtió en una atracción turística después de que Hollywood empezara a rodar películas de James Bond en las que aparecían tiburones.

Arriba: Junto a las líneas perfectamente desarrolladas del tiburón, los humanos parecen fuera de lugar. Sin embargo, el privilegio de observar a un tiburón es una experiencia por la que la gente está dispuesta a pagar.

A pesar de que este tiburón martillo gigante *(Sphyrna mokarran)* come otros tiburones, no muestra ningún interés por el buceador que se acerca a fotografiarlo. Estos grandes tiburones están extremadamente bien adaptados para la depredación. Sus ojos les permiten mirar simultáneamente a objetos diferentes, mientras que su extraña cabeza actúa como un detector de metales, captando impulsos eléctricos diminutos en el agua que los rodea.

Algunas personas acaban
trabajando cerca de los tiburones en el marco de estudios
científicos. El intrépido volun-
tario Mike Braun empuja
un tiburón tigre *(Galeocerdo
cuvier)* por el agua para
reanimarlo después de some-
terlo a un proceso de medición
y etiquetaje como parte del
programa de investigación de
la Universidad de Miami en las
costas de las Bahamas.

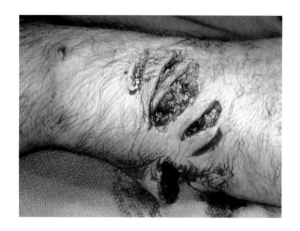

VÍCTIMAS DE TIBURONES

Bethany Hamilton nació para surfear. Es la personificación del sueño americano. Al igual que las demás personas que aparecen en este capítulo, es miembro de un club muy selecto, aunque nadie quiera formar parte de sus integrantes. Bethany fue víctima del ataque devastador de un tiburón que le costó un brazo y casi acaba con su vida.

Tenía 13 años. Una mañana de octubre de 2003, Bethany se dedicaba a su actividad favorita: surfear en las costas de la North Shore de Hawai. Lo que pasó ese día cambió su vida. Bethany esperaba una ola con la mano izquierda meciéndose en el agua. No llegó ni siquiera a ver el tiburón. Todo se volvió borroso, según recuerda. «Sucedió en pocos segundos. Recuerdo como el agua a mi alrededor se tiñó de sangre. Luego vi que me había arrancado el brazo casi hasta el hombro de un mordisco.»

Bethany es una joven apasionada por la vida, así que logró borrar de su mente el más mínimo pensamiento funesto. Afortunadamente, la gente que había en la playa actuó con presteza y logró salvarle la vida. Un amigo usó la correa de una tabla de surf para hacerle un torniquete en lo que había quedado reducido a un muñón.

En esta ocasión el culpable resultó ser un tiburón tigre. La gente del lugar dio muerte al tiburón que según ellos era el responsable, afirmando que la marca de sus dientes correspondía a la perfección.

La historia de Bethany la catapultó instantáneamente a los titulares. Su extraordinaria recuperación y su deseo de volver al agua la convirtieron en una celebridad. Todo el mundo quería saberlo todo sobre ella. Apareció en programas televisivos de todo Estados Unidos y fue entrevistada sin pausa por periodistas de todo el mundo. Bethany no culpabiliza en absoluto a su atacante. Su filosofía, sencilla pero madura, es: «Pues si te ha tocado…»

Argumenta que es inútil preguntarse constantemente «¿qué habría pasado si…?». Aunque algunas personas que han recibido heridas de este tipo pierden la confianza o se esconden del público, Bethany rehizo su vida alrededor del deporte que más ama con la ayuda de su familia y sus amigos. Incluso escribió un libro sobre sus experiencias, *Soul Surfer* (Surfista de corazón). Bethany ha superado su terrible accidente, se niega a llevar brazo ortopédico y compite con entusiasmo en campeonatos de surf. Sin embargo, supo desde ese día que iba a ser

conocida para siempre como «la chica surfera a la que un tiburón arrancó el brazo».

El porqué fue atacada es otra cuestión. Los tiburones no son asesinos premeditados. Si pensamos en sus presas habituales y en cómo las ven ellos, y luego nos fijamos en el aspecto que debe de tener un surfista para un tiburón que nada por debajo, probablemente resolveremos que una tabla de surf con brazos o piernas colgando de los lados se parece a una foca o una tortuga. Teniendo en cuenta que una buena parte de las víctimas de los tiburones son surfistas, los científicos están convencidos de que la mayoría de los ataques son sencillamente casos de identificación errónea. En muchos de los incidentes el tiburón deja en paz a la víctima después del primer ataque, porque es algo ajeno a su dieta habitual.

Chris Sullivan, un profesor de Newquay, en Cornualles, fue una de esas víctimas. Él también había estado surfeando con sus amigos durante las vacaciones en Noordhoek, en Sudáfrica. El día era magnífico y el agua, cristalina. De repente, Chris percibió bajo él una gran sombra que no presagiaba nada bueno. Era un tiburón blanco. Chris sabía que tenía que salir de ahí, pero el tiburón le tiró de la pierna y lo arrastró junto con su tabla de surf. Chris comentó con humor: «Le di un par de puñetazos de niña. Noté como la pierna se desgarraba, pero los dientes eran tan afilados que no sentí dolor».

La herida de Chris era grave, pero tuvo suerte de no tener ningún hueso roto y de que la hemorragia no fuera demasiado abundante. De hecho, tras tomar una ola que lo llevó a la orilla, consiguió subir por la playa, con el traje de neopreno manteniendo unida la pierna desgarrada. Al igual que Bethany, tuvo suerte de que hubiera gente cerca que reaccionó a toda velocidad para atender sus heridas. Aunque podía ver el daño, estuvo riendo y bromeando todo el tiempo. Chris recibió unos 200 puntos en el hospital y su recuperación ha sido

Páginas anteriores

Página 68: Este mordisco fue infligido por un tiburón de 2 m de longitud.

Página 69: Bethany Hamilton vuelve a sonreír después de recuperarse del ataque de un tiburón mientras surfeaba en North Shore, Hawai.

casi completa. Su historia también despertó un enorme interés mediático. Ambas historias tienen como nexo en común una pasión por el océano que ha empujado de nuevo a Chris a las aguas que bañan su hogar, en Cornualles, zona de peregrinación para los surfistas en el Reino Unido. Obviamente, no puede evitar reaccionar cuando ve sombras extrañas en el agua, pero luego aplica rápidamente la lógica que le dice que «aquí no hay tiburones», o por lo menos sólo inofensivos tiburones peregrino.

Los tiburones siempre habían entusiasmado a Chris. Ahora afirma sentirse más fascinado que nunca y trabaja activamente para difundir el mensaje de que «los tiburones son unos animales fascinantes y misteriosos que necesitan de nuestra comprensión». Su búsqueda de un mejor entendimiento le llevó a contactar con otra víctima de un gran blanco en Sudáfrica, con quien ha llegado a desarrollar una singular pero estrecha amistad.

Craig Bovim salió a capturar langostas para la comida de Navidad el 24 de diciembre de 2002. El clima en Scarborough era horrible. Había un fuerte oleaje y la visibilidad en el agua era escasa, pero Craig estaba decidido. Mientras buceaba con tubo, un tiburón blanco de gran tamaño empezó a nadar junto a él, tan cerca que pudo distinguir al detalle cada una de las cicatrices y marcas de su cuerpo. Los tiburones suelen tener cicatrices producidas durante el apareamiento, o como Craig cree que era el caso, como consecuencia de peleas con otro macho.

Luego lo perdió de vista. «Estaba realmente asustado. Luego vi la aleta viniendo directa hacia mí como una lancha.» El tiburón le mordió con fuerza en los antebrazos y empezó a tirar de él hacia el mar. Sin saber cómo, Craig consiguió librarse de los afilados dientes del tiburón, aunque desgarrando un gran pedazo de músculo del brazo. También recibió una mordedura grave en la pierna. Para cuando llegó a la orilla, estaba perdiendo muchísima sangre. Tras varias operaciones, Craig ha recuperado totalmente la funcionalidad del brazo izquierdo pero solamente el 30% del derecho. Craig afirmó que hasta el ataque que casi le costó la vida, nunca había pensado demasiado en los tiburones, hasta el punto de avergonzarse por su ignorancia.

Dado que ha pasado una gran parte de su vida en el agua, es consciente de que estadísticamente las posibilidades de encontrarse con tiburones eran a la fuerza mayores. El ataque tuvo un gran impacto en su vida y desde entonces lucha por cambiar la forma en que la gente trata a los tiburones. Se opone vehementemente a la moda de las inmersiones en jaula usando carnada para atraerlos. «Antes había cazadores de trofeos que mataban tiburones. Ahora tenemos a gente haciendo negocio a costa del turismo relacionado con ellos. Demos el siguiente paso y empecemos a observar a los tiburones de una forma pasiva, sin atraerlos con cebo.»

Craig Bovim y Chris Sullivan consideran que no podemos estar seguros de que alimentar artificialmente a los grandes blancos no vaya a modificar su comportamiento y así, a su vez, incrementar el peligro para los humanos. «Por eso no deberíamos arriesgarnos», argumenta Craig. Aun así, el riesgo es ínfimo. Estadísticamente, es más fácil que nos atropelle un coche o que nos caiga un rayo encima que recibir la mordedura de tiburón.

Tony White, un galardonado fotógrafo submarino inglés, fue a tomar imágenes de un increíble fenómeno llamado «sardine run» (carrera de las sardinas) en Sudáfrica. Se produce cuando miles de millones de estos pequeños peces emigran hacia el norte a lo largo de la costa, desatando un frenesí alimentario en miles de depredadores, desde delfines y pájaros marinos hasta atunes y tiburones.

Tony estuvo a punto de perder un brazo a los pocos minutos de su primera inmersión. Su error, según él, fue colocarse encima de una «bola» de peces (una «bola» se forma cuando miles de peces nadan pegados entre sí para protegerse). Cuando un tiburón cobrizo arremetió contra la bola para darse un festín, atrapó el brazo de Tony con tanta fuerza que lo sacó del agua. Tony salvo el brazo gracias al rápido traslado a un hospital en el que los médicos estaban acostumbrados a tratar con heridas infligidas por tiburones. Tony también tuvo que superar su miedo a volver al agua para continuar ejerciendo su profesión. Pero lo consiguió, y está firmemente convencido de que «el tiburón no me atacó, sólo me mordió por error, es así de sencillo».

Pese a todo el bombo publicitario y el sensacionalismo que se ha asociado durante años a las víctimas de tiburones, suelen ser precisamente ellas las primeras en defenderlos.

Probablemente la víctima de tiburón más famosa de todo el mundo sea el australiano Rodney Fox. En 1963 un tiburón blanco lo hirió de una forma tan terrible que fue un auténtico milagro que sobreviviera. Necesitó 462 puntos. Se enorgullece de que «desde entonces he dedicado la mayor parte de mi vida al cuidado, la conservación y la investigación del gran tiburón blanco».

Es inevitable que más personas sean víctimas de tiburones en el futuro. Sin duda, el miedo y la fascinación ancestrales que siente el hombre por el tiburón no van a desvanecerse, pero tal vez nuestro conocimiento del rey del gran azul mejorará y nos ayudará a preservar el territorio del tiburón.

El fotógrafo submarino Tony White estaba capturando imágenes de un frenesí alimentario en una bola de sardinas cuando un tiburón cobrizo *(Carcharhinus brachyurus)* lo atrapó por el brazo derecho y lo sacó del agua. Hubo que grapar el brazo de Tony alrededor del codo. Su recuperación ha sido excelente y él insiste en que no fue un ataque. El tiburón, sencillamente, «me mordió por error».

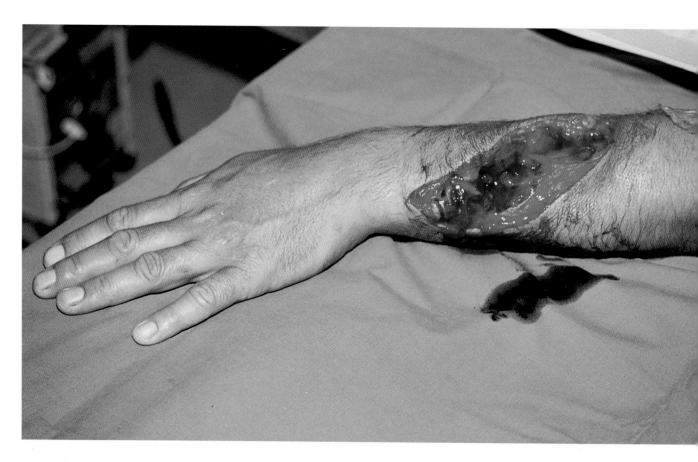

Un gran blanco estuvo a punto de arrancarle los brazos a Craig Bovim mientras buceaba cerca de su casa en Sudáfrica. Actualmente emplea su tiempo en hacer campaña para lograr un enfoque del turismo con tiburones más respetuoso con el medio ambiente.

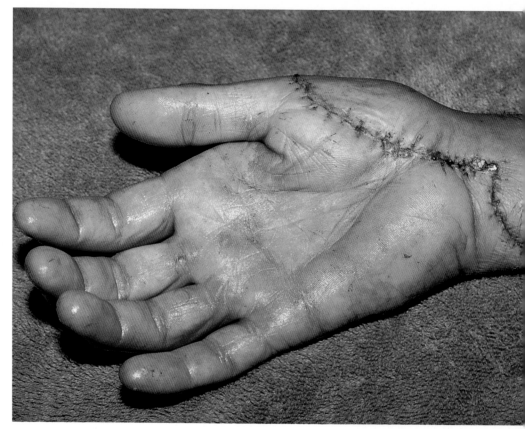

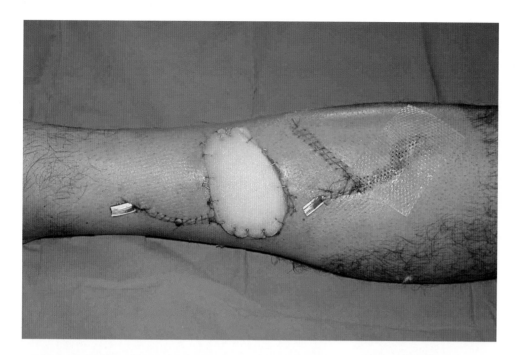

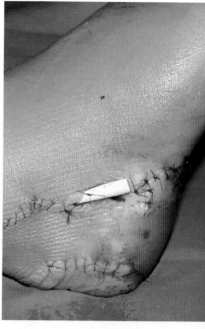

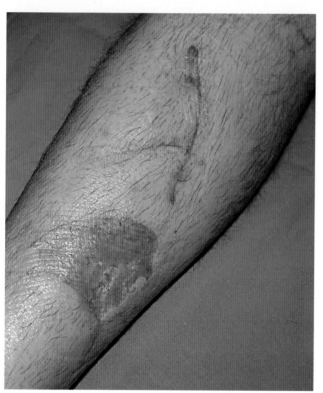

Chris Sullivan necesitó 200 puntos después de que un gran blanco le mordiera la pierna mientras surfeaba en Sudáfrica. Su fascinación por los tiburones aumentó después del accidente. «Son unos animales increíbles y misteriosos que necesitan de nuestra comprensión», afirma. Derecha: Chris y su pareja, Barbara Robinson, posan con la tabla de surf y el traje de neopreno mordidos por el tiburón.

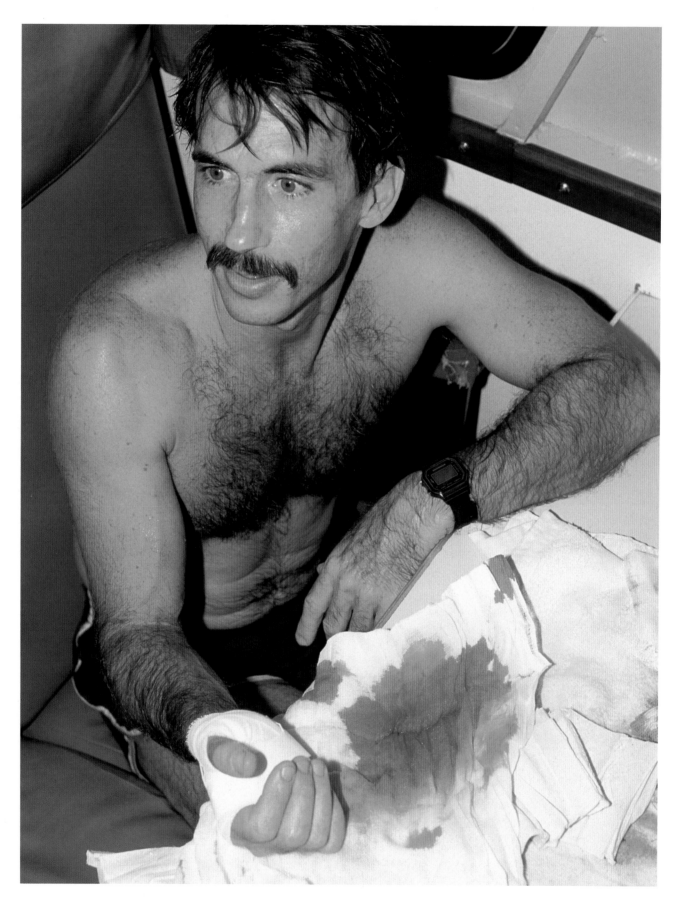

Página anterior: El fotógrafo submarino Doug Perrine recibe atención médica en la mano tras ser atacado por un tiburón coralino en las Bahamas en 1988.

Derecha: Vista desde abajo, la silueta de un surfista es parecida a la de una foca o una tortuga, lo que probablemente lleva a los tiburones a atacar por error.

Abajo: El australiano Rodney Fox se hizo famoso en todo el mundo tras ser víctima en 1963 del ataque de un tiburón blanco que casi acabó con su vida. Necesitó más de 460 puntos en los brazos y el abdomen. Desde entonces, ha luchado infatigablemente a favor de los tiburones, concienciando a la gente sobre su lugar en la jerarquía del océano e intentando parar las matanzas llevadas a cabo para producir sopa de aleta de tiburón.

EL GRAN BLANCO

Cuando Steven Spielberg rodó *Tiburón*, creó un monstruo. Aquel inquietante «chan-chan, chan-chan chan-chan» llegó a simbolizar todos nuestros temores en relación con el carnívoro más famoso (aunque es discutible que sea el más peligroso) del océano, el gran tiburón blanco.

Cuando uno ve esos grandes dientes, afilados como cuchillas, sobresaliendo de la enorme mandíbula, cuesta creer que en realidad se trata de un pez grande con un cerebro relativamente pequeño.

El tiburón blanco también es conocido como jaquetón blanco y muerte blanca. Son, sin duda, una raza aparte, supertiburones. Han evolucionado durante más de 100 millones de años, afinando sus instintos asesinos hasta el punto de que no resulta extraño que no tengan rival en el primer puesto de la cadena trófica marina.

Un ejemplar de tamaño considerable puede superar los 6 m de longitud, con un peso de más de 2.000 kg. Los científicos calculan que el tiburón blanco es capaz de ejercer una presión letal de casi 4 toneladas por centímetro cuadrado cuando muerde algo. Según historias y leyendas populares se han encontrado tiburones blancos gigantes de más de 9 m de longitud. Una criatura mítica de las costas de Sudáfrica era supuestamente tan grande que recibió el sobrenombre de «submarino con dientes».

Casi todas las imágenes que vemos de tiburones blancos nos muestran una enorme boca abierta, el hocico ensangrentado, ojos negros como el carbón y, lo más terrorífico, unos dientes puntiagudos, tan afilados que pueden cortar la carne más dura como si fuera mantequilla. No cabe duda de que son asesinos aterradores, capaces de infligir terribles heridas. La película *Tiburón* exacerbó la fama de devorador de hombres del animal. El argumento era convincente. Se basaba en la idea de que algunos tiburones acechaban y cazaban deliberadamente a víctimas humanas con una violencia casi gratuita. La truculenta imagen de un nadador solitario siendo despedazado, como ha ocurrido en la vida real, conmocionó al mundo. El impacto de la película, basada en el *bestseller* homónimo de Peter Benchley, fue tan profundo, que desató la matanza de miles de tiburones a manos del hombre, alimentada por un miedo irracional que llegó al paroxismo.

Sin embargo, afortunadamente los ataques perpetrados por tiburones blancos son infrecuentes. De

Con un indiscutible aspecto de asesino, un gran blanco muestra su níveo vientre mientras nada cerca de la superficie.

de persecución. Por ello, el tiburón pone en práctica un juego táctico de paciencia y caza oculto en las oscuras profundidades. El tiburón busca señales que indiquen la presencia de una víctima, tal vez una que esté desprevenida volviendo a la orilla después de alimentarse.

Cuando llega el momento oportuno, el tiburón sale disparado hacia la superficie para golpear a la foca con tal ímpetu que saca al animal totalmente fuera del agua. Si el ataque inicial tiene éxito, la foca está condenada. Después, el tiburón se limita a nadar en círculos alrededor de su presa hasta que devorarla resulta seguro. Lo último que necesita un tiburón es que una foca herida le lastime los ojos. Algunos tiburones poseen una membrana nictitante, que cubre y protege el ojo en los momentos finales del ataque; sin embargo, el gran blanco carece de ella y sencillamente gira el ojo hacia atrás para salvaguardarlo. Es posible que el tiburón tenga que realizar varios ataques, potencialmente peligrosos, antes de terminar con éxito la cacería.

Los grandes blancos pertenecen al grupo de los tiburones lámnidos, que incluye al marrajo dientuso, con forma de torpedo. Son de sangre caliente, lo que significa que pueden generar calor corporal adicional en sus músculos. Dado que los grandes blancos suelen encontrarse en aguas relativamente frías, un aumento de 10°C en la temperatura corporal, que incrementa su velocidad y capacidad de reaccionar con rapidez, puede suponer la diferencia entre el éxito y el fracaso durante la persecución de un mamífero de sangre caliente.

Los programas de televisión suelen mostrar grandes blancos atacando botes o mordiendo las jaulas de los tiburones. Durante mucho tiempo, este comportamiento fue considerado una prueba de que atacaban indiscriminadamente. Pero los estudios han demostrado que en las fases finales de la cacería el tiburón confía en su hocico hipersensible, salpicado por diminutas cavidades capaces de detectar débiles impulsos eléctricos. Por ello, es posible que en el último minuto el tiburón se sienta abrumado y confuso por el campo electromagnético, relativamente fuerte, de la embarcación o de la jaula metálica. El instinto le dicta que muerda con

hecho, el promedio de víctimas mortales por ataque de tiburón es de 12 al año. La naturaleza de los ataques y nuestra morbosidad hacen que estas muertes den la vuelta al mundo con todo lujo de detalles.

Los estudios sobre el comportamiento de los tiburones en el sur de Australia, Sudáfrica y la costa oeste de los Estados Unidos (especialmente en California) han mostrado una gran variedad de patrones de conducta que aportan pistas sobre cómo y por qué atacan de la forma en que lo hacen.

Los grandes blancos han demostrado ser criaturas increíblemente sigilosas. Su dieta básica consta normalmente de focas y leones marinos, así como de peces como el atún, ricos en grasas. Pero las focas son extremadamente ágiles, unas rivales más que dignas para su monstruoso agresor en caso

Páginas anteriores

Página 76: El tiburón blanco (Carcharodon carcharias) en todo su esplendor como depredador rey.

Página 77: La aleta dorsal del tiburón blanco basta para desatar el pánico entre los bañistas cuando emerge cerca de una playa.

fuerza, y dado que los tiburones carecen de lengua, ésta es también su forma de «catar».

Lo cierto es que los humanos no son demasiado «sabrosos» para los tiburones, ya que su contenido graso es muy pobre. Por ello, es errónea la creencia de que los grandes blancos son los principales devoradores de hombres. De hecho, tan sólo son responsables de entre el 10 y el 20% de los ataques de tiburones a humanos. Actualmente, los ataques de tiburones se consideran casos de identificación errónea. La película *Tiburón* perpetuó el mito del «asesino a sangre fría» y, hasta el día de hoy, los escalofriantes gritos de los nadadores mientras eran devorados vivos por un tiburón blanco siguen resonando en nuestros oídos.

Cuando Peter Benchley escribió *Tiburón* se sabía muy poco sobre los escualos. Admite con franqueza que su obra contribuyó a demonizar a los tiburones y actualmente no sería capaz de escribir la misma historia, sabiendo lo que sabemos sobre ellos. Buceador desde hace muchos años, Benchley ha disfrutado de la emocionante experiencia de estar cara a cara con el gran blanco, aunque desde la seguridad de una jaula en las aguas del Pacífico. Considera que los encuentros con este animal fascinante han sido una lección de humildad. No puede retroceder en el tiempo, pero más de tres décadas después del estreno de la película, espera que su legado imperecedero sea su colaboración en la lucha para salvar al vilipendiado e incomprendido tiburón blanco de la persecución y la demonización.

Peter Benchley, el autor de *Tiburón*, a escasos metros del animal que ayudó a demonizar. Volviendo la vista atrás, afirma que no escribiría el mismo libro y se declara un ferviente entusiasta del predador supremo de los mares.

Arriba: Espectacular salto de un tiburón blanco de 1.400 kg. Los expertos creen que el tiburón carga hacia su presa desde las profundidades a tal velocidad que acaba efectuando un impresionante salto en el aire. Se puede animar a los grandes blancos a saltar remolcando una simple tabla de madera recortada con la forma de una foca desde la popa de una embarcación.

Derecha: Los tiburones poseen varias hileras de dientes. Las hileras superiores se usan para cortar, mientras que los dientes inferiores sujetan a la presa. Cuando pierden dientes durante un ataque, las piezas de las hileras posteriores se desplazan hacia delante para reemplazarlos, como si se tratara de una cinta transportadora. Se estima que un tiburón puede llegar a usar hasta 5.000 dientes a lo largo de su vida.

Los grandes blancos suelen
lucir las cicatrices de luchas
anteriores por la supervivencia. Las hembras pueden
mostrar heridas infligidas por
los machos, que les muerden
durante el brutal apareamiento, y los machos también
muestran a veces las cicatrices
de sus luchas por la suprema-
cía dentro de su comunidad.

Tragedia en medio de un banco de jureles que intentan escapar de las fauces del implacable depredador.

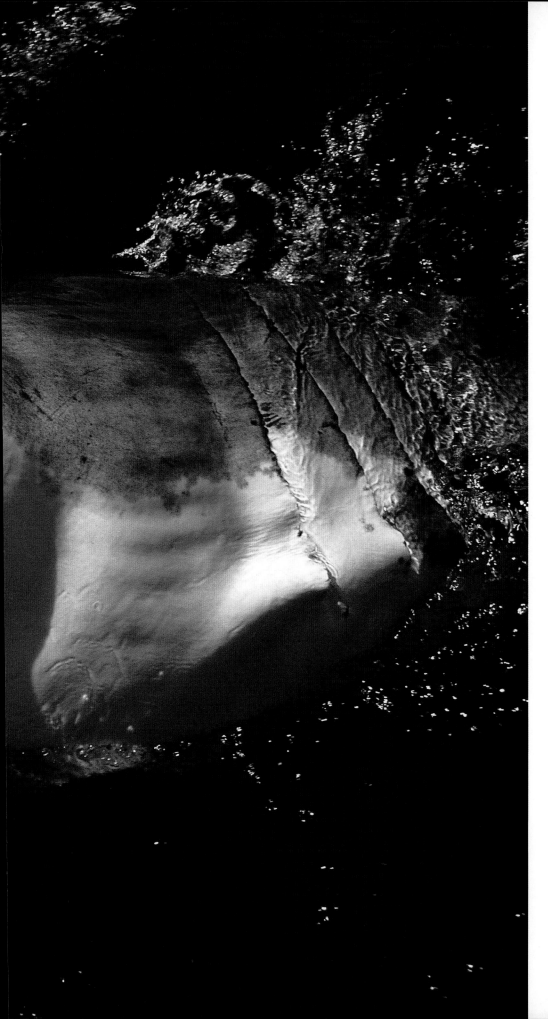

No es infrecuente que los
grandes blancos saquen la
cabeza fuera del agua. Es lo
que se conoce como «oteo»
y demuestra una vez más la
agilidad del tiburón a la hora
de buscar comida, ya que
los mamíferos que nadan en
la superficie son parte de
su dieta.

Cuando los grandes blancos
se preparan para atacar, usan
primero la vista para localizar
a la presa. A medida que se
acercan, giran sus negros ojos
hacia atrás para evitar que
los mamíferos marinos los
dañen con sus afilados dientes
o con sus garras. Es entonces
cuando los electrorreceptores
situados en el morro, extremadamente sensibles, toman el
control para lanzar con precisión el ataque definitivo sobre
sus víctimas.

Arriba: La coloración azul grisácea de este tiburón, unida a su vientre blanco, proporciona un excelente camuflaje en el mar. La gente que ha sido atacada por grandes blancos suelen verlos sólo en el último momento. Son criaturas muy sigilosas.

Derecha: Una de las imágenes más impresionantes que pueda haber es la del mítico tiburón blanco apareciendo a pocos metros de uno. Una jaula es la mejor protección frente a mandíbulas capaces de ejercer una presión de 4 toneladas por centímetro cuadrado.

Los estudios realizados sobre los tiburones blancos echándoles carnada han contribuido a descartar algunos de los mitos que los rodean. De hecho, se cree que son animales sociales que viven en grupos con una jerarquía establecida, lo cual se torna especialmente evidente al observarlos mientras comen. Las hembras suelen ser más grandes que los machos y por ello son el sexo dominante.

Las impactantes imágenes de Douglas David Seifert de un gran
blanco en las costas de Guadalupe (México) muestran por qué la
mayoría de nosotros siente un miedo innato por estos inmensos
carnívoros marinos. En un mundo tan profundamente alterado por
el hombre, el tiburón blanco es el recordatorio más formidable
de una jungla marina en la que sólo el más apto sobrevive.

ÍNDICE ALFABÉTICO